The Master's Call!

Dennis Cramer

The Master's Call

Nine simple questions to identify your ever-changing call

Dennis Cramer

A Word in Season
VOLUME I

The Master's Call:
Nine Simple Questions to Identify Your Ever-Changing Call
Dennis Cramer Ministries
2308 West Mountain Ave.
South Williamsport, Pennsylvania 17702
Phone: 570-320-7757
E-mail: denniscramer@suscom.net
Website: www.denniscramer.net

Copyright 2005

ISBN 1-886296-34-0
Printed in the United States of America
First printing 2005

Author's note: The Scripture verses and passages in this book were not taken from any one version or translation of the Bible. Unless otherwise noted, combined portions of various translations were used to more accurately portray or expand on the intended meaning. All biblical quotations, however, were taken from recognized, authentic, and published Bible translations.

To order books contact:
Arrow Publications
P.O. Box 10102
Cedar Rapids, IA 52410
Phone (319) 395-7833
Toll Free: (877) 363-6889 (U.S. only)
Fax: (319) 395-7353
Website: www.arrowbookstore.com.

Dedication

To all who have experienced the
spiritual pain and pleasure of having the
Master's *ever-changing call*
of God upon your life.

Contents

Key Scripture

"Brethren,
Be even more diligent...
Take all the more care...
Make all the greater effort...
Do your absolute best...
Be all the more earnest...
Be zealous...
Exert yourself to make your election
and (ever-changing) calling sure,
  If you do this,
You will never stumble...
You will never make a slip...
You will never come to grief."

2 Peter 1:10

From the Author
The Global Shift Is On!

I believe that you, the reader, as a living member of the church of Jesus Christ, the pillar and ground of the truth, with all of her wonderful spiritual diversity and vitality, are about to experience yet another dramatic shift in your spiritual life — a classic spiritual paradigm shift. It will be a powerful, permanent paradigmatic shift away from the spiritually old and routine, and into the spiritually brand new and exciting! I predict you will never, never, never be the same!

A Brand New "Thing" Means A Brand New Call

Isaiah wrote,

> "Nothing compares to what I'm going to do [with **you**] says the Lord! Behold, I am going to do *a brand new thing* [with **you** personally]. See, I've already begun [to do it]. Don't **you** see it?" (Isa. 43:19).

All willing believers, just like you the reader, will soon be dramatically swept away into something so new and so wonderfully exciting that it will literally take your spiritual breath away! And I say, bring it on, Lord Jesus! Please, take my breath away! Do that brand "new thing" in me!

The key, however, to properly responding to this global paradigmatic shift in the church will be this: It will be absolutely necessary for you to embrace quickly a brand new call upon your life. That's right — a brand new call, *the ever-changing call of God upon your life*. Everything in your spiritual life is about to change — nothing will remain the same! Are you up for the challenge? Are you willing to change? Are you willing to move forward? The choice is yours to make. Don't make the wrong one.

Your old call is being replaced — wonderfully, powerfully, and permanently replaced by God Himself. You didn't do anything wrong. You didn't sin, and you didn't miss God. Your call is just being replaced. God Himself is changing your call. What an awesome thought! Your years of obedience are finally paying off. You are being promoted.

There was nothing wrong with your first call, but it is now old and outdated. In one sense it is irrelevant. It is used up. It has run its course. It enjoyed its season. It served its purpose for its pre-appointed, designated time. Previously you did what God wanted you to do and when He wanted you to do it. That's what a genuine call really is: Faithfully doing the will of God, whatever it is, when and where He wants you to, and doing it with joy. So the good news is you've done the will of God. Again, you're being promoted.

> A genuine call is: Faithfully doing the will of God, whatever it is, when and where He wants you to, and doing it with joy.

What is a Genuine Call?

But now, there is more to do — a lot more. You will need a new call, an *ever-changing call of God* to accomplish what He wants you to accomplish today. This is the purpose of your ever-changing call: To do something great for God today, tomorrow, and to bring Him the greater and greatest glory beginning now.

Clearly, God is moving on, and so is His call upon your life. It is high time that you catch up to the ever-changing call of God and ardently pursue with renewed passion and spiritual vigor the revealed will of God for your life from this point on. Yes, it is time for you to go on the offensive again. Whether you are sixteen or sixty-five, it is time to go on the offensive. It is time once again, today, right here and right now, to make your election and calling sure.

———

This is the purpose of your ever-changing call: To do something great for God today, tomorrow, and to bring Him the greater and greatest glory beginning now.

———

New Vision, New Power, New Call!

"Where there is no [new, future] *vision* the people (inevitably) perish" (Prov. 29:18).

Allow me to be lovingly blunt. You need a new vision for your life. You need new empowerment, and you need a new call. You need something new to hold on to. Something you can "sink your spiritual teeth" into again. You know this. You feel this. You need a new vision for your life, new power for your life, and a new call for your life. You need these now!

Yes, you were faithful and obedient in the past to fulfill your old call. You clearly did your part, and God is very, very pleased. But that was then, and this is now. However, to even consider the possibility of such a dramatic shift away from the familiar, from the routine, may seem quite disturbing at first. I understand. This may seem like such a daunting task that you would rather run and hide than deal with this much change, but it must be done. Your spiritual destiny depends on it.

If you are honest with yourself you know this is exactly what is happening to you, and in you. You are changing on the inside. You are changing spiritually. Your call is being "dislocated" and "relocated" at the same time. Again, the shift is on! It is time for you to respond.

Apparently, God has summoned you to accomplish something great for Him. Otherwise, you would not be reading this book at this time. However, you will accomplish this only through your ever-changing call.

You see, your ever-changing call may not be as stationary or fixed as you may have previously thought. Anything stationary is characterized by little or no movement. Your call however, is just the opposite. It is all about movement. Specifically, your call is about forward movement.

The truth is, the nature of your *ever-changing call* is probably the opposite of stationary — the direct opposite. Your *ever-changing call* is shifting. In fact, it is shifting dramatically as God wants you to go in a completely new direction. Therefore, your responsibility is to adapt to it, to change with it, to go with God. I believe the shift is on! God is moving. Your call is moving, too. Are you?

➤

Anything stationary is characterized by little or no
movement. A call from God is never stationary. Never!

➤

Clearly, it is time for you to advance! Again, you are being promoted. God's promotion for your life will mean both greater responsibility and greater authority. Both are a part of His ever-changing call on your life.

New Means New — Really New!

"....for you have *not* [ever] passed this way before." (Josh. 3:4)

I believe the Lord Jesus is speaking to you right now. He is saying with great excitement and anticipation: "New call, new call, new call!" He is saying that a new and even more exciting, *ever-changing call* is coming upon you, even wonderfully overtaking you and replacing your old outdated call.

Be honest with yourself. You are certainly not the same believer you were five years ago. You are not even the same believer you were six months ago. Why? Something is up. Something is in the air. What is it?

Your *ever-changing call* is changing again, and hopefully you are changing with it. Your *ever-changing call* is changing you from the inside out. Change with it, and you will meet God in a marvelous new way as you experience Father God on His terms again — to accommodate His will for your life.

In the process, (which you must volunteer for), you will become more spiritually effective, and more spiritually useful to Him again. Once again you will become His true servant — putting His best interests first.

Consequently, your sense of spiritual satisfaction and significance will once again be powerfully restored. You will feel spiritually reinstated and spiritually rejuvenated. You will feel spiritually renewed and relevant as you experience a deep new sense of spiritual accomplishment.

↩

*Respond properly to the **ever-changing call of God**, and you will feel restored, reinstated, rejuvenated, renewed and relevant all at once!*

↩

Updated And Upgraded!

" today ... your inner man is being renewed...." (2 Cor. 4:16)

Again, your ever-changing call is changing and changing big time. Whether you realize it or not, you are going from faith to faith, from glory to glory, *and from call to call!* In other words you are in process. You are on a journey. There is an incredible exchange taking place in your life.

Old outdated calls are being removed, and new even better contemporary *ever-changing calls* are replacing them. You are being spiritually altered, modified, and turned into something totally new and even more deadly to the kingdom of Hell. This change is precisely what you have been praying for. This is your time, your season, and your coming out!

Something's Up?

" *you* ... be transformed...." (Rom. 12:2)

An awesome spiritual transformation or reconfiguration of enormous proportions is ongoing inside you right here, right now.

> You are being wonderfully, powerfully updated and upgraded by the Spirit of God.

Something's up! You feel it deep, deep within your spirit. You cannot identify it quite yet, but you know it is there — this feeling simply cannot be denied. You have tried to ignore it. You have tried to shut it off. You may even have inadvertently attempted to cast it out! It's like a hunger, a hunger in your spirit that just won't go away.

↩

A call of God is like a hunger that just won't go away.

↩

What you may have falsely identified as a work of the devil has in fact been a sovereign work of Almighty God. It is so new, so unprecedented in your life that you simply did not and could not recognize it. However, try as you may, the feeling simply won't go away. This hunger persists. Why?

You are being wooed. You are being courted. You are being pursued. Like a persistent suitor, the call of God is relentless in its divine purpose. Its purpose is to catapult you to the next level of service to God.

↩

The ever-changing call of God is like a persistent suitor.
It woos you, it courts you, it pursues you.

↩

It Feels Like...

Let's specifically analyze how you've been feeling lately. See if any of this applies.

- You feel spiritually uncomfortable, clumsy, awkward, exposed, even naked.
- A sort of spiritual constipation has gripped you. You no longer feel free.
- You feel spiritually vulnerable, borderline insecure, and you don't like it. You've lost your former spiritual identity.
- You're having doubts where you never even use to have questions. You're thinking: What have I done wrong?

↩

I'll tell you exactly how you feel:
You feel spiritually naked!

↩

Believe me, I understand. It is happening to "cutting-edge" believers just like you all around the world. It is a sense of deep inner transformation and substitution that is inescapable. Something is being removed, and something is being replaced. You know it, you feel it.

Exactly what is this feeling? You are experiencing a type of spiritual discomfort or pain. I mean real inner pain. And like all forms of pain, even mild pain, this pain hurts. It genuinely hurts. But there is a clear divine purpose for this "spiritual" pain.

Sorry, No Pain, No Gain!

"....until Christ is formed in *you*...." (Gal. 4:19)

The good news is there is always gain after pain. Great pain means great gain! Please don't worry. What you are feeling is not some form of punishment or penalty. No, not at all! All is well. *Your call is just changing.*

Your new call is like a baby. It is almost finished passing through the birth canal. A birth is taking place. It is a blessed event! Your new ever-changing call has just arrived. Now it is time to name the baby! It is time to name the ever-changing call of God upon your life.

You Are Being Spiritually Repositioned

Again, the good news is, what's going on inside you, and what's about to come out of you, (the birthing), is not the devil. You don't need deliverance. You don't need counseling. You don't need prayer. You are just being repositioned by the hand of Almighty God.

All you need is some definition and some clarity. You need to know what this repositioning is all about. You need to know what God requires of you today and you have every right to know this.

What is going on inside you are the multiple spiritual, emotional, and even physical effects of the *ever-changing call of God* upon your life.

⟶

You are changing because your call is changing.

⟶

You Are Being Spiritually Prepared

"To every thing there is a *season* and a purpose...." (Eccles. 3:1)

I believe you are about to enter one of your most exciting seasons. It will be a new season that is unparalleled and unprecedented in your personal history with God. Consequently, as you read this book you are experiencing deep, dramatic, paradynamic change. God is preparing you. Why? Every new season requires new preparation.

You Are One of a New Breed!

Put on the new man, which is renewed in knowledge after the image of Him who created you (Col. 3:10).

From all this change a new and dangerous atypical breed of believer is emerging. You are one of these new emerging atypical believers — a new deadly, dangerous type of believer with a new *ever-changing call* upon his life. To put it simply, you are going to the next level.

➤

Every new season requires new preparation.

➤

You are being led of the Holy Spirit into new territory. It is a new place in the kingdom where you will no longer be a spectator or a follower. It is a place where "each joint will supply" something necessary and even critical, to the full operation of the body of Christ (Eph. 4:16). This includes you. You have something to "supply."

Are you ready? Are you prepared to participate? Can you handle this next level? Apparently God believes you can. Otherwise, He wouldn't be calling you to it! You are one of the "new breed."

Your New Great Awakening?

Paul wrote, "....and do this, knowing the time, that now it *is high time to awake out of sleep*, for now our salvation is nearer than when we first believed" (Rom. 13:11).

"Awake you who sleep, and Christ will give you light" (Eph. 5:14).

My sense is that you, like many in the body of Christ, are being awakened from your sleep. This may not be the beginning of the last great awakening on earth, but it may be the beginning of the next great awakening in your life!

As in all earlier "awakenings", heads are going to turn, both among the religious and non-religious, the saved and the unsaved. Both the world and the church will never be the same.

> This may not be the beginning of the last great awakening on earth, but it may be the beginning of the next great awakening in your life!

What does this awakening mean for you personally? What should you do? What should your practical response be? How can and will you participate?

You must awake, you must shake off the slumber upon your spirit. You must wash the spiritual "sleep" out of your eyes. Your spiritual awakening depends on it. I hear the Lord saying to you, "Get up, son!" "Get out of bed, daughter!" "Let's get moving, children!" "There's work to be done, Church!" "It's a new day and a new hour!" It is time to embrace your *ever-changing call.* It is time to work the works of God!

Again, Paul wrote, "The night is far spent, *the day is at hand.* Let us cast off the old and put on the new." (Rom. 13:12).

This may be the beginning of the next great awakening in your life! Are you ready? Have you, are you, casting off the old and putting on the new. Notice that you are to do both the "casting off" and the "putting on." God leaves both responsibilities up to you.

⤴

*There's work to be done, Church! It's a new day and a new hour!"
It is time to embrace your ever-changing call.*

⤴

What I Want For You

"I cease not to ... make mention of *you* in my prayers" (Eph. 1:16).

I want you to begin to experience this new *ever-changing call of God*. I want you to begin to experience it right here and right now — in all its fullness and power — to own it and to make it yours. I want you to act on it — and to get it right. I want you to be incredibly clear on exactly what God wants you to do for Him today and tomorrow — not last week, last month, or last year.

So let's explore together, in clear, simple, every-day language exactly how you can identify God's awesome *ever-changing call on your life*. Let's discover together how you can successfully act on it right here and right now so you, too, can make your election and calling very, very sure. Amen!

Dennis Cramer

Introduction

The apostle Peter, anointed by the Holy Spirit of God, commanded all Christians to "make their election and calling sure." This was not a mere suggestion but a clear authoritative divine command — a command inspired by the Holy Spirit. This command became a part of the canon of Scripture.

In fact, he told them to be "even more diligent." That is, to be more bold, more spiritually aggressive, and more spiritually opportunistic in pursuing this kingdom imperative. Peter was commanding with apostolic authority that these early Christians become offensive minded. He wrote, "Brethren, be even more diligent to make your election and [personal] calling [ever] sure" (2 Pet. 1:10).

Why was the issue of one's ever-changing call so important to Peter? Why did he include this strong apostolic admonition in the very first chapter of his second letter?

> "Brethren, be even more diligent to make your election and calling [ever] sure" (2 Pet. 1:10).

Your True Calling

The Apostle Peter knew something many Christians today have forgotten.

Peter knew that your call is not a true call unless it can be successfully identified and acted upon. It is a lifelong process. He knew that each and every believer, whether then or now in the twenty-first century, has a unique call upon his life. He knew that this ever important call must be clearly discerned or identified and then faithfully executed or fulfilled by the individual to whom it was given. He knew that to miss your calling was to miss God. Peter knew! Do you?

Peter knew that your "ever-changing call" is where your identity, security, purpose, and destiny lie. It is why you were put on earth in the first place. Your call is the real reason you were born and the real reason you were born again. It is the very reason for your existence. It is not just part of your life. Your call is your life — your entire life. This is why it is absolutely necessary for each believer "to make his election and calling sure" each and every day. Your spiritual future literally depends on it. Not to mention your eternal reward!

So, What is Your Call?

It is time to settle the issue. Notice that Peter was not warning just certain church leaders or those in "full-time" or paid positions within the church. No! He was warning all believers. All means all.

He was warning all the "brethren," which included all the men and women of God in that region, to make their calling sure and to firmly establish what God wanted them to do. Today, God wants you to settle the same issue and stand fast in the will of God for your life too.

Please listen. God is saying the exact same thing to you right now: Have you settled the issue of your calling? Have you, are you, doing the present will of God? If you are not, then be warned!

~

To miss your calling is to miss God.

~

What Does Your Calling "Sound" Like?

" ....except there be a *distinct sound* ... how will it be known? (1 Cor. 14:7).

▪ **A call of God should be like a clear sound.** It should be identifiable and clearly distinct from all other distracting noises in your life. It should be a sound you hear in your spirit that is clearly measurable and clearly manageable to you.

▪ **A call should be well defined, clearly identifiable, and something that is workable, practical, and applicable to your life** — a perfect sound and a perfect fit just for you. After all, your call was made just for you.

―

Don't worry. God has given you the spiritual capability to hear your call — to distinguish it from all other distracting sounds.

―

It should have definable perimeters or boundaries you can "hear" so you can know what God wants you to do and what He does **not** want you to do. Hearing and knowing what is His will and what is not His will is imperative. These are the *do's* and the *don'ts* of your call. In this sense the call of God both releases and restricts you. You are called to do some things, and called **not** to do other things.

The awesome "sound" of your call will activate you and motivate you to do great things for God. The "sound" of your call should be nothing less than the driving force behind how you live your entire life. Yet it is a unique sound, a highly personal sound that only you can hear for you. You must be the one who has an ear to hear it. Do you?

―

The "sound" of your call should be nothing less than the driving force behind how you live your entire life.

―

Are You Moving Ahead?

Your call should be understood as:

▪ Continually changing you for the better ... radically repositioning you!

- Constantly keeping you in a state of supernatural flux ... fluid and flowing, whether you like it or not!
- Always moving you ahead ... onward and upward ... futuristic in nature.

Therefore, some critical questions must be asked:

- Are you prepared to be repositioned by it?
- Are you sufficiently fluid and flowing toward it?
- Are you progressing with it or are you lagging behind?

Without a clear and full knowledge of one's ever-changing call, the possibility of stumbling or forfeiting one's destiny in God greatly increases. Peter even linked making one's calling sure to successfully entering the kingdom of God. That is, to being a true success in one's service to God.

> **A call is not a call unless it can be acted upon.**

"Make your election and calling sure ... for in doing so an entrance will be made for you into the everlasting kingdom of our Lord Jesus Christ" (2 Pet. 1:11).

The implication is clear. You may even jeopardize your eternity with all of its various levels of reward if you do not do this one thing, namely making **your ever-changing calling** sure.

God only ever moves forward. And so does His call upon your life.

In the Greek

In 2 Peter 1:10 the Greek word (*spoude*) translated "diligent" or "diligence" means: to do so speedily, to dispatch with eagerness, to earnestly fulfill, to make haste in making your calling sure.

Next, the Greek word (*bebaios*) translated "sure" in this same verse means to make stable, firm, fast, secure, steadfast to find God's pace or gait (walk) for your life." Peter told them that if they would make their calling "sure" they would "never stumble."

The word "stumble," in the Greek, means you will not be tripped up, you will not err, and you will not fail. If you will make your calling sure, you will never fail! You will not and cannot stumble! What a precious promise from God: Walk out your call and you walk in success!

Have You Inadvertently "Stumbled?"

Have you, are you, stumbling in your service to God? Have you or are you failing to meet His and your expectations for your life?

Have you become spiritually dormant, drained, spiritually impotent, and spiritually ineffective? Is the *ever-changing call of God* upon your life an "unsure" rather than a "sure" thing?

> If you are diligent, speedy, eager, and earnest to make your call sure, stable, firm, fast, and secure, you will never stumble, trip up, err, or fail!

Do you feel stale? Are you bored? Are you tired of the same old, same old, of your Christian experience? Are you sick and tired of being sick and tired?

Making your *ever-changing call* sure (stable, firm, fast, and secure) can change all of that. What do you have to lose?

↩

A call is progressive, it is always moving ahead.

↩

Pick Yourself Up!

Have you tripped up or erred? Have you spiritually stumbled? Has the call of God on your life become a very unsure thing? Has the ever-changing call of God moved on in your life, and you have lagged behind? Don't worry, you are not alone. However, it is high time for you to act. It is time for you to wake up. It is time for you to get up and stand up.

↩

It is time for you to wake up, get up, and stand up,
and be counted among the called of God!

↩

Your Problem Is A Common One

Your problem is really two-fold. It is, however, a problem that can be easily corrected. First, you have probably made the same mistake tens of thousands of other believers have made regarding their call. You have mistakenly perceived the call of God as a static thing, something that is at rest, something not moving, something that makes little or no progress and no forward motion, something which stands still.

You thought your calling was something that does not change, something that remains constant throughout your Christian experience, something that is somehow fixed in time, something rigid and unchanging. That's your problem! In fact, it's the opposite. That's right, the opposite!

Your ever-changing call of God is not static — it is extremely fluid.

Your ever-changing call is something very fluid. It constantly flows, it continually runs, it moves unceasingly, it changes regularly, it evolves daily. It even grows in its intensity and scope. It is more like a river in motion than a pond at rest. It flows rather than stands still. It is more a variable than a constant. This means it is more apt to change than to remain the same. To move rather than to stagnate.

Irrevocable?

What about Paul's writings on this subject? He wrote to the church at Rome that the call of God is an "irrevocable" part of the believer's life (Rom. 11:29). I couldn't agree more! Irrevocable simply means the ever-changing call of God originally placed upon your life will not be removed or withdrawn by God. However, it does not mean your call was introduced into your life fully developed and completely matured. Not at all!

Your ever-changing call comes in stages, segments, pieces, and portions

Your *ever-changing call* will be introduced into your life in well thought out stages or segments. These supernatural pieces or portions are progressively distributed into your life in a series of subtle supernatural deposits rather than one sudden overwhelming lump sum.

Consequently, you must recognize and respond to each new stage, receiving each new "deposit" as it is presented to you. Accepting or rejecting these "deposits" is always a decision that only you can make. It is the difference between obedience or disobedience, the difference between success and failure in the kingdom of God. This is what your call is really about anyway — strict compliance or obedience to the revealed will of God.

So, what about you? Are you willing to obey the ever-changing call *of God* upon your life? Are you ready for the next stage? Are you prepared for God's next supernatural deposit in your life? Trust me, it will be worth it!

＜

Do you feel pregnant in your spirit? Good! That's probably your ever-changing call trying to be birthed.

＜

It's Just Like a Baby

I've got really good news for you. If you are reading this book, whether you are a woman or a man, you are pregnant! There is nothing wrong with you. You are just pregnant. You are pregnant in your spirit, and your pregnancy is about to come to an end as it runs its course and accomplishes its intended purpose.

Pregnancies are always about births. And as with all pregnancies a "baby" is about to be born! You, dear brother or sister in Christ, are about to give "birth" whether you are a woman or a man. How exciting for you!

It is a fact. You are pregnant right now with a new *ever-changing call*, and that call is soon to be birthed. I predict it! I prophesy it! A release is imminent.

Here's how you feel right now: You feel something heavy on the inside of you — in your spirit. It's a good "heavy," a bit uncomfortable at times perhaps, but still an essentially good feeling. Like a beautiful pregnant woman, you feel life. Something is actually living on the inside of you. You, too, are a carrier, a servant-carrier of a soon-to-be-born new, *ever-changing call of God.*

―

The "life" you feel on the inside may be your
ever-changing call attempting to be born!

―

You are about to become a spiritual parent. How sobering! How wonderful! Your life is about to change forever. Something is about to be added to your life which never existed before. A whole new chapter, an entire new era is beginning. There will be both new responsibilities as well as new joys. Even if you've given birth before, even if you've responded to earlier calls of God upon your life, you are about to give birth again. Congratulations!

Back to the Baby

Like a precious infant at birth, your call might not arrive looking particularly cute. After all, the birthing process of your call can be spiritually and emotionally messy, even a bit traumatic. Don't worry; you'll be fine.

Still it is an exciting and blessed event to be sure, but a tough delivery nonetheless. Eventually, your call will mature and develop over time. It will experience its own infancy, then its own childhood, its own adolescence, and ultimately its own adulthood.

A Baby Has To Grow

Remember, your call potentially supplies you with all the spiritual abilities you will need to change lives and to wreck untold havoc on the devil, thus promoting God's kingdom in your generation.

However, your ever-changing call will usually be introduced into your life in very small, very well thought-out stages or segments. These series of individual supernatural deposits are not made in one sudden or overwhelming lump sum because a call is like a baby.

A baby must grow slowly and steadily because normal growth just takes time. So does your call. Therefore, don't expect sudden growth spurts or quick advancement within your call. Sudden or instantaneous growth would be the exception not the rule. Growth spurts can happen, but they are rare.

↔

*A baby must grow, and growth
takes time. So does your call.*

↔

Re-fired Not Re-tired!

Your *ever-changing call* will also require strict maintenance or upkeep for it to remain supernaturally contemporary, truly anointed, and permanently effective.

It may even require periodic "slow downs" or periodic "shutdowns" in order to increase its longevity and life span. Please note that "slow downs" and "shutdowns" are good and necessary. During these pre-ordained "slow down's" and "shut downs," God often re-fits you to further accommodate His constantly evolving plan for your life. This does not mean that God takes anything from you. Not at all! He does not revoke the calling. In fact, it means just the opposite. He is not retiring you. He is actually re-firing you spiritually! He is adding to your life, not taking away from it. It means He is giving you more supernatural grace and more and better supernatural gifts to help you carry out His will for your life.

(You Are) Deadly, Deadly, Deadly

God often refits and re-tools you to make you an even more deadly weapon in His arsenal. Yes, you are God's weapon! His call on your life makes you deadly and dangerous. You are an open threat to the kingdom of hell. What an honor!

However, far too many believers seem to lose their edge in the supernatural realm. They seem to fall off the pace of what God is doing on the earth. Why? They enter a kind of spiritual time warp because they failed to discern that their call changes, morphs, or alters its original form. Their call changes, but the believers don't — a tragedy repeated daily in the body of Christ. The key is to change with your call. The key is to be re-tooled, thus re-fired not retired.

You may have mistakenly thought you figured out 25 years ago what God wanted you to do with the rest of your life, yet you have not re-examined or re-visited that critical decision since then. This is a common mistake but nonetheless a big mistake!

God does not collect antiques! He wants and expects you to be modern — to be able to relate to what He is doing today. A believer becomes a spiritual antique when he fails to navigate the many twists and turns within his *ever-changing call*. It is true that antiques have value. But most have no practical usefulness. Don't become an antique. God wants you to have both value and usefulness in his kingdom.

Are You a Spiritual Antique? I Hope Not!

You must understand exactly the definition of " a process." A process is a series of changes or actions directed toward a specific goal. The process of making your calling sure will involve thousands of personal decisions, hundreds of course changes, and dozens of major examinations throughout your life. Again, it is a lengthy process and not a single, solitary event.

What Is A Call Of God?

"....who He predestinated He also *called*...." (Rom. 8:30).

Exactly what is a call of God? How does one recognize it? A call of God is a divine apprehension. The apostle Paul wrote he had been "called" supernaturally apprehended by the will of God for a specific, divine, perfect kingdom purpose.

Making your ever-changing call "sure" is not a single event, but a lifelong process.

Paul wrote, "I press on that I might lay hold of that [divine call] for which I have been [personally] *apprehended*" (Phil. 3:12).

A call of God is therefore a supernatural invitation, a summons, an appointment, a demand from God upon a life. It's a supernatural thing! It's an honor of the highest order. It's an unspeakable privilege. When Almighty God "calls" someone, He is demanding in the strongest of terms the lifelong service of that person. But there is a cost. *An ever-changing call of God means service to God and man at the expense of self.*

—

*An ever-changing call of God means service
to God and man at the expense of self.*

—

The Bible Says:

▮ You are a partaker of a heavenly *calling*! (Heb. 3:1).
▮ You have been *called* with a holy *calling* (2 Tim. 1:9).
▮ You must behave in a worthy manner based on your *calling* (2 Thess. 1:11).
▮ You have a *call* of God upon your life, which will require great effort to reach. A great personal prize awaits those who press into it and possess it (Phil. 3:14).
▮ You have been *called* to a glorious future. (Eph. 4:4 Amp.)
▮ You were *called* by none other than Jesus Christ. (Eph. 1:18).
▮ You were not *called* based on human qualifications. (1 Cor. 1:26).
▮ You were *called* with an irrevocable call. (Rom. 11:29).
▮ God will faithfully fulfill your *call*, for He's the One who initially issued the *call*. It was His idea, not yours. (1 Thess. 5:24).
▮ He *calls* you as a unique individual, even *calling* you by name. (John 10:3)

—

You will truly succeed in God only where you are truly called of God.

—

Sometimes, It's Audible — Usually, It's Not

A call carries with it a very specific responsibility from God that you and only you can fulfill — a "custom fit" call.

In the Old Testament, God sometimes called people in dramatic fashion by speaking audibly, allowing them to physically hear his voice. This was the impressive method God used to call Moses and Samuel. Others, like Abraham, Sarah, and Jacob, were all given new names signifying their unique call. Each of these calls carried with them a specific responsibility that God expected each individual to assume.

God may or may not call you audibly. However, the essence of a call, whether it is audible or not, is the same from time immemorial.

In the New Testament the act of calling people to a kingdom task continued. For example, **the apostle Paul** was audibly called by Jesus Christ to a ministry position. On the famous Damascus road, Jesus Christ personally called out, "Saul, Saul, why do you persecute me?" And then apprehended Saul (soon to become Paul) to a spectacular earthly apostolic ministry. This was Paul's calling — his divine summons.

> A call of God is a divine summons, an appointment, a divine demand from God upon your life.

Jesus also called many of **His personal disciples** by giving them new names. Examining the gospels reveals many such New Testament calls. Even today, though we do not audibly hear from God or speak to Jesus in person, God is still apprehending individuals, His 21st century disciples, for various kingdom tasks. We understand these supernatural apprehensions as "calls of God."

An Unspeakable Privilege

Your call is an unspeakable privilege, the greatest of earthly honors.

The Eternal God of heaven and earth has decided to "employ" you. You have been hired by heaven! You work for God! Awesome, isn't it?

But your call can change or mutate — even radically. The **apostle Paul** began his ministry as the prophet Saul (Acts 13). In this example, a prophet's call evolved or supernaturally mutated into an apostle's call. Saul became Paul. A prophet became an apostle.

Stephen started out called as a deacon but eventually walked in the calling of a powerful New Testament minister and martyr. **Phillip** also started out in obscurity only to be called later to a powerful New Testament ministry of evangelism.

In two particularly tragic cases a call was forfeited or lost due to gross disobedience as seen in the self-destructive lives of **King Saul** and of course **Judas Iscariot**. Both these men were originally called but disobeyed God and suffered great loss. It is a terrible waste when a man or woman of God walks away from their call. Don't **you** do it!

So What About You?

Every one of God's earthly children has a unique *ever-changing call* upon his life — a very specific divine purpose — God's perfect personal plan. This clearly includes you! You are not the exception — no one is! Yes, you are called — personally, individually, uniquely!

Specifically, you are called to do something great for God! Your calling includes greatness because your calling includes your destiny.

Your employer may overlook you for a well-deserved promotion. Your pastor may have his favorites, and you may not be one of them. Even your friends and family may not clearly recognize your potential greatness in God. But God does! Within every genuine call of God there lies potential greatness for you. It may be in a dormant stage at this time, but it is time to revive it, to resurrect it, to activate it, to resuscitate it. It is time to make your calling "sure." It is time to act and act decisively. Why? The glory of God is at stake!!!

The "greatness" of your calling will always translate into much glory and honor for the One who called you in the first place. Remember, your call is all about Him! It was given to you by Him, through Him, because of Him and for Him. Your *ever-changing call* is all about the Lord Jesus Christ.

God has not ignored you, and you have not been disqualified. In fact, you may not have even begun to fulfill your call! So what do you do next? Simple: you start asking some key questions.

Nine Simple Questions About Your Call

I now offer you nine simple yet powerful and profound questions to

A great God has placed a great call upon your life to bring Him great glory. Amen!

ask yourself. Remember, God does not want to tease or torment you regarding your call. Not at all! He fully intends to answer each of these nine questions. With all His heart He desires to communicate His expressed will so you can make your "election and calling sure." After all, He is the one who commanded you to do just that, and He would never have commanded you to do something that you were incapable of doing. So begin now to make your calling sure. He will do His part. Will you do yours?

Please do not ask these nine questions of your neighbor, your friends, your pastor, or even your spouse. Ask them of yourself. This book is about **your call**, not someone else's. I have the utmost confidence in God that He will answer you very, very specifically.

Above All, Please Be Honest

The honest answers to these nine simple yet profound questions will help you to

- accurately isolate and identify
- properly receive and release
- supernaturally activate
- and successfully act upon....

the unique *ever-changing call of God* on your life today. The end result will be a wonderful new spiritual direction, a strategic new vision, an unprecedented level of greater supernatural power and effectiveness in your ministry. You are about to be born again, again!

Born Again, Again?

Yes, indeed! You are about to be born again, again! You are now about to experience a quantum leap forward in your service to God, a whole new beginning, a fresh start. Once again you will be "about your Father's business," and only your "Father's business" (Luke 2:49) Once again your joy will be full! Once again you will have true peace of mind. Once again you will know a deep sense of spiritual and emotional satisfaction, an abiding sense of personal accomplishment, fulfillment, and significance. All this will come about only with knowing and doing the will of your Heavenly Father! You will feel like you were just born again, again! Let's begin!

"The deep sense of personal reward your ever-changing call provides — that deep personal sense of satisfaction it gives — literally feels like heaven on earth!"

— *Dennis Cramer*

Question 1

As a Christian, what rewards you the most?

alls can and will drastically change, and their rewards can and will change with them. So, often times, new rewards can point to new calls. Follow the reward, follow that deep sense of personal satisfaction and spiritual fulfillment, go in that new spiritual direction, go with the new supernatural "grain," go with the Holy Spirit's "flow," and you may discover *your ever-changing call!*

Constantly ask yourself, "what new thing that I'm doing for God seems to reward me the most?"

What I Did Not Ask You

I did not ask you what it is you want to do. I did not ask you for your list of personal likes and dislikes. I did not ask you for your "shopping list" of things you would like to try. I did not ask you what you think might be fun — not at all. This is not about you finding some kind of new hobby or pastime, something with which to amuse or entertain yourself. This is a much more serious choice.

> New rewards always reveal new calls.

Instead, I am asking you to look at something else. I am asking you for an honest appraisal of something different, something more serious in nature. I am asking you to try and locate the single source of greatest spiritual reward in your life. Notice I said "spiritual" reward.

Spirit vs. Flesh

A reward of this nature is experienced in your spirit. Your flesh may hate it, but your spirit-man will love it. Why? It is your calling. Your spirit-man always loves the call of God upon your life. At the same time your flesh, your lower nature, will equally hate it. At least initially.

So here is the good news. If your flesh rebels against the same thing your spirit-man seems to love, you have probably found your call! It is often your spirit-man who experiences the true reward of your calling. It is your spirit-man, (your inward God nature), that experiences true excitement, even exhilaration, at the call of God upon your life.

You "feel" the reward of your calling on the inside — in your spirit-man.

So, no matter how strange it may seem to your flesh, ask yourself:

- What is it that I do for God that makes my spirit-man feel like I want to do this for the rest of my life?
- What seems to supply my spirit-man with the greatest joy?
- Where does my spirit-man experience the deepest sense of peace as far as service to God is concerned?
- What excites and exhilarates my spirit-man the most?

These answers may point to a new and *ever-changing* call upon your life.

I Know, I Know, I Know How You Feel...

I know how you feel. I've felt this way myself many times. I know what you are thinking. You're thinking: But what I'm doing makes no sense! I've never done this before! This is all too new to me. True, I'm experiencing joy, but at the same time I feel very inadequate. I'm experiencing great peace, yet I'm nervous about this whole new direction!

Is this normal? Yes! You're definitely headed in the right direction. Will you at times feel stupid? Yes! Will you at times want to quit! Yes! Will you feel spiritually clumsy at times? Absolutely! Still, you can expect eventually to realize a great sense of reward as you pursue your new *ever-changing call*. Don't quit!

Men Go Fishing — Women Buy Shoes

Different kinds of activities offer different kinds of rewards. There are secular or casual activities and their less important reward. I'm referring to spiritual activity, however, and that which you do for God and the subsequent spiritual reward. That is, the unique spiritual reward, premium, or prize that God gives to you when you obey His *ever-changing call*.

Faithfully fulfilling your *ever-changing call* has a unique and incredibly satisfying sense of reward attached to it. It is a reward like none other. It is a deep and abiding sense of gratification that cannot be experienced through any other activity. God reserves this rare, even unique sense of reward only when you fulfill His specific will for your life. This occurs when you carry out God's pre-determined plan for you as you "work the works of God" that only you can work.

I love to fish. I mean really love it. I could fish all day. I could fish for the rest of my life. I mean just fish, nothing else. As a result of this leisurely activity, I experience a type of reward because it's fun and I love doing it. But this is a very different kind of reward than the kind God gives to those who fulfill their *ever-changing call*.

My beautiful wife loves to shop. She loves to hunt for bargains, and she's good at it. Shopping is fun for her, and there's nothing wrong with scouting out good deals. Consequently, she feels a certain sense of reward when she finds a bargain. But, there are different types of reward attached to different kinds of activity. Fishing has its reward, and shoe shopping has its reward. But there is another kind of reward.

God has a deeper, more satisfying type of reward for you.

Here's How I Feel

I can only explain to you how I feel as I fulfill *my ever-changing call*. When I'm finished ministering, I'm exhausted. I'm exhausted, but tremendously rewarded. I'm wonderfully spent, but powerfully fulfilled. I'm finished, but enjoying the greatest sense of personal reward I have ever known. No other activity in my life has ever made me feel so fulfilled, so honored, so good, so right, so clean on the inside, so effective, so complete. Why? It's my calling. I'm experiencing the unique reward that God has attached to my particular calling. So will you!

This is what you need to be on the lookout for: The unique sense of accomplishment that follows when you fulfill God's call on your life. It's like no other feeling on earth. In fact, my theory is you are feeling a little bit of what heaven actually feels like! It feels amazing!

By Definition

A reward is simply the result of accomplishment — something offered for legitimate service or achievement. To be rewarded is a part of life — even the Christian life. God rewards those who obey Him and carry out His will, who fulfill His call upon their lives.

A reward is a perfectly good thing, an honest thing, a well-deserved thing. God often gives you the greatest sense of reward where He wants you to spend the most time. It is where He wants you to focus your attention and where He wants you to make the greatest impact for Him. He attaches personal and spiritual reward where He calls you. If you can locate the source of greatest spiritual and personal reward in your life, you may have discovered your *ever-changing call*.

God Rewards the Called

What is it that you do for Jesus that floats your spiritual boat and pushes all your spiritual buttons? What provides you with your greatest sense of personal satisfaction and fulfillment? What gives your life true meaning? What ended your search for significance as a believer? The answers to these questions may help you to begin to discover or re-discover *the ever-changing call of God* upon your life.

God often gives you the greatest sense of reward where
He wants you to spend the most time.

What rewards you the most might not make sense to you in many ways. You may not even understand why a particular activity or ministry makes you feel so fulfilled, but none of this matters. Your mind might not grasp what your heart is telling you. In spite of all the signals to the contrary, you find yourself doing something for God that you never thought you would enjoy. It may be something you never thought you were good at or something that you certainly never thought previously you were called to do.

What's going on, you may ask? Your call is changing. You find yourself tremendously rewarded serving the Lord in areas you were never trained for, have no experience in, and still feel a little clumsy doing.

I Love This Stuff!

Still, there is no denying that your sense of personal and spiritual reward is off the scale! You absolutely love this new thing you're doing for God. Would you like to know why? Because God has called you to do it.

A believer, who finds himself walking in the call of God for his life is going to love — I mean **really** love what he does. You will love what you are called to do.

After over 26 years of ministry, I can honestly say, "I love this stuff!" When you finally respond to the ever-changing call of God upon your life and begin to fulfill it, you, too, will cry out, "I love this stuff!"

The Three R's

What is it that you are currently doing for God that provides you with your greatest sense of personal and spiritual reward, return, and results? Personally, there is nothing I do that rewards me more than my ministry. Nothing that I do gives me a greater sense of return, and nothing that I do produces greater results for the kingdom of God. Why? It's my calling.

Where do you experience your three R's: Your greatest sense of reward, return, and results? This may be the calling you should pursue and the direction you should take. This may be the new direction of your *ever-changing call.*

- **Reward** — Where are you the most spiritually satisfied by satisfying the spiritual needs of others?
- **Return** — Where are you the most spiritually successful by making others spiritually successful?
- **Results** — Where are you the most spiritually empowered by spiritually empowering others?

Although there is a crown with every call — a significant spiritual witness or feeling of inner reward, you must remember your call is not primarily about you or even for you. *Your ever-changing call* is about others and for others. So enjoy the crown, but be ever vigilant to be faithful to the call.

There is a crown with every call!

Paul Found It!

Apparently, the apostle Paul found what provided him with his greatest sense of personal and spiritual reward. He experienced the reward, return, and results of his calling. He too experienced his crown. He said in his letter to the Philippians that he had found something so incredibly rewarding that every other human endeavor in his life paled in comparison to this single source of reward. He wrote that every other pursuit in his life he "counted as dung" and as "rubbish," or as "loss" when compared to this one "thing" that he did for God. He wrote that he was forgetting everything else in his past and "reaching" with all his might to grasp that which God had for him.

Paul was referring to the call of God upon his life — *an ever-changing call* like the one on your life! He wrote that he was pressing toward this goal to win a prize, to get his reward (Phil. 3:14). He realized that Jesus Christ is not only the One who gives the reward, but Jesus Christ is the reward! I believe Paul loved what he was doing. I believe ultimately you will, too!

Go With How You Feel

The call of God is definitely changing in your life. Perhaps it is changing even more radically than you even realize. You may find yourself occupying a place of ministry or service to God that you never dreamed you would hold. And yet there is no denying the tremendous new sense of inner reward you are experiencing.

The *ever-changing call of God* upon your life makes no sense to you at all, but you sure do love how it makes you feel! Sometimes you need to go with how you feel, not with what you think.

Sometimes you need to go with how you feel,
not with what you think.

For Example...

For forty years you've worked in the nursery on Sunday mornings. That's all you have known. That's all you've wanted to do. You've always genuinely loved little kids. But now you're outside the church, working in the poorer neighborhoods, helping to feed the less fortunate, and you love it! It feels different, but it sure feels good.

Or, you've never really been evangelistic in nature, but now you're out on the streets, part of a church sponsored program to reach the lost, and you love it! Again, it feels very different, but very good.

Maybe you never thought you had a prophetic bone in your body, but now the pastor has put you in charge of training up the prophetic people in your church, and you love it!

Even five-fold, ascension gift, full-time, Ephesians 4:11&12 ministers are changing. I mean really changing. Pastors are becoming apostles; prophets are becoming evangelists. And they love it!

Eventually, you will love what you are called to do.

No matter how totally different the *ever-changing call of God* upon your life may seem at first, eventually, you will love what you are called to do.

Question 2

As a Christian, what is it that (wonderfully) depletes you the most?

In chapter one we discussed the deep spiritual and personal rewards of *the ever-changing call of God* upon your life: The "prize" that awaits all obedient servants of God (Phil. 3:14).

By carefully analyzing the source of this reward, you will be better able to distinguish your new *ever-changing call of God* and determine what it is that God wants you to do for Him today.

Now you must examine the other side. You must allow the pendulum to swing in the opposite direction. Now you must look not at what your call gives to you, but what it takes from you — what it requires of you both physically, and more importantly, spiritually. What "uses you up" the most?

> **A new source of reward indicates a new call of God.**

Point One: Physical Fatigue

I'm not talking primarily about being physically depleted or physically fatigued. Any legitimate call on your life will certainly involve physical effort that will result in physical fatigue. Fatigue is good and simply means you have worked hard for God. Even Jesus was fatigued at times.

Normally it takes me two full days just to recover physically from one of my typical itinerant trips. There's nothing wrong with being tired and needing rest. In fact, it's a good indicator that I've done the will of God. It's a good sign I'm moving ahead in the *ever-changing call of God* for my life.

I've never worked so hard as I do right now. I accept this. I know my call requires great effort, but it is an effort I am honored to give. However, I do not mean that what you do for God should leave you physically over-extended, overly exhausted, or on the verge of some kind of total physical or emotional breakdown. Not at all.

What you do for God will deplete you physically. That is a fact. One simple but effective way to determine the new direction of your *ever changing call* is to think about what new spiritual activity or ministry — what service to God (whatever it may be) seems to fatigue you, to make you weary? Your greatest sense of physical fatigue often indicates to you the area of your greatest responsibility in the kingdom of God.

⌒

There's nothing wrong with being tired and needing rest.
In fact, it's a good indicator that you've done the will of God.

⌒

Even the Apostle Paul Got Tired

Paul the apostle made a statement in 1 Corinthians 15:10 that always catches my attention. It is a curious little reference that sheds some light on the first point of this chapter.

He wrote, "I labored more abundantly than all [the other apostles]."

What did he mean? It's simple. Paul was writing about hard work, which is pure physical effort. Here, the word "labor" in the Greek meant, "fatigue, hard work, to be wearied." Paul worked very hard at his call. So should you.

Point Two: Spiritual Fatigue

Let's look at what I call spiritual fatigue, and ask yourself these questions:

■ What is it that drains you spiritually?

■ What siphons off your spiritual batteries?

■ What activity depletes your anointing and draws upon your spiritual gifting?

■ What and where is the greatest demand placed upon you spiritually?

> **You will never know greater fatigue than when you are operating in your ever-changing call.**

■ What is it that you do for God that leaves you wonderfully emptied and satisfyingly drained?

■ What leaves your spirit fatigued to the point where you experience the most spiritual tiredness?

The answers to these questions help to pinpoint the direction of *your ever-changing call of God.*

Your Spiritual Tank — Your Spiritual Battery

God gave you a spiritual tank and a spiritual battery, which is the unique spiritual capacity to retain and release certain gifts and abilities through your life. His purpose in giving you this spiritual tank and battery was to empty the tank and drain your battery. That's right. God gave you these things to empty and drain them. "Empty and drain" are good kingdom words. Your spiritual tank was designed to be emptied, and your spiritual battery was specifically designed to be drained.

↝

You have not been called to be abused by Jesus.
You have been called to be used up for Jesus.

↝

Just as I recommend that you carefully analyze where you are physically depleted, you should also more carefully analyze where you are spiritually depleted, fatigued, or "used up" for Jesus. I didn't say "abused by Jesus," I said "used up for Jesus" in that place of service to which God has called you.

This careful examination of new areas of spiritual fatigue involves that wonderful draining of your anointing and can indicate to you any new direction of your *ever-changing call of God.* New areas of spiritual fatigue that make a demand upon your gifts, clearly reveals new ministry responsibilities along with new and more exciting kingdom work for you to assume.

Yes, your physical man and your spiritual man will get tired as you pursue your *ever-changing call of God*. This is one evidence you are in the will of God and fulfilling the call of God.

—

Ever been spiritually "tapped out" for Jesus? Good! You are probably fulfilling your call.

—

From Personal Experience

I have faithfully fulfilled the call of God on my life, and I have never known greater spiritual fatigue. I, too, must refill my spiritual "tank" each and every time it is drained. I, too, must recharge my spiritual "battery" the same way you do. Like me, if you can locate where your anointing seems to be the most discharged, the most released, the most used up, this may be the direction of your *new ever-changing calling*. You were given your anointing for it to be used up — for God to use you as He pleases — for His glory!

Your spiritual tank was designed to be emptied, and your spiritual battery was designed to be drained.

Ask yourself this question: What is it that constructively uses you up spiritually? Specifically, what is it that you do for God that leaves you spiritually spent, wonderfully emptied, and marvelously drained for Jesus? The answer may indicate where your *new ever-changing calling* is taking you.

Ask yourself:

▌ Where does my Jesus use me up spiritually the most?
▌ Where does my Jesus empty my spiritual tank the most?
▌ Where does my Jesus drain my spiritual battery the most?

It makes sense if you think about it for a moment. Your gift, your talent, your anointing, your spiritual grace or ability was given to you for one purpose: For God to use it — for Him to use it *and you* up.

When He has finished using you, you are done as well. You go from the supernatural back to the natural. You become merely human again. You are no longer super-human as when God's Holy Spirit was moving through you. This transfer back to the normal and back to the natural, leaves you spent, empty, finished. This is normal. All called people feel this way. You just need to go and rest somewhere. You just need to refill your tank and recharge your battery.

Remember, even Jesus got tired, both physically and spiritually. Even He needed to get away and rest periodically. Even He needed to withdraw to refill His tank and re-charge His battery. He too experienced both physical and spiritual fatigue just as you do. It comes with the *ever-changing call of God.*

Jesus would never call you, and then abandon you.

The Best Shepherd

Jesus is much more than just a Good Shepherd. He's the *best* shepherd — the best shepherd you will ever know! He is an outstanding caretaker, the Great Shepherd of His sheep (Heb. 13:20).

Although He will often require much of you, He is always there to protect you, to provide for you, and most importantly to *restore* you both physically and spiritually. He does not call you and then abandon you.

The Lord is your personal shepherd. You will not be in want, in lack, or neglected in any way. He will allow you to lie down, to rest and eat when needed.

The Lord is your personal shepherd. You will not be in want, in lack, or neglected in any way.

He will lead you on. He will be with you. He will comfort you. He will prepare a table of all that you need. He will refresh you regularly by anointing you and by re-anointing you as well.

Your cup, the over-all quality of your life, will overflow. And, if that were not enough, God's goodness and mercy — His personal pleasure with you — will follow you, and you will forever live in His presence.

Now that is a Great Shepherd. Whatever call He may require of you, He will provide all you need to faithfully fulfill it. Why does He do all this for you? He has destined you for success, not failure, in your ever-changing calling.

"When you think about the ever-changing call of God on your life, you should start thinking like a lottery winner!"

— *Dennis Cramer*

Question 3

As a Christian, what would you do differently for God if money were not an issue?

I understand that most believers will probably never receive any financial compensation for their ministry. They will probably remain faithful kingdom "volunteers" throughout their years of service to the Lord. So some might not grasp the importance of this third question if they never expect to be paid for any of their ministry in the first place.

In this chapter, I'm not referring to being paid for ministry. I'm asking you (perhaps a volunteer) to consider what you would do *right now* if you never had another financial concern the rest of your life.

What if all your bills were paid forever, and money would never again be a part of the equation? What would you do for Jesus *right now*?

Sound impractical, illogical, and impossible? Is such a venture far too dangerous for you? Good! That's why I wrote this chapter. I want you to begin to think dangerously!

Thinking Like A Lottery Winner!

I'm asking you to begin to think like a lottery winner! A lottery winner does what's in his heart (hopefully for good!). As soon as he won the lottery, he stopped using his brain so much and started listening to his heart — his inner voice. He started following his dream.

I'm asking you to listen to your heart and to follow your dream. I'm asking you to listen to your inner man — the one God is trying to get in touch with.

Lottery winners become fearless. They begin to think and act differently when they are freed from financial fear. Why? They are no longer forced to make decisions based on their restricted circumstances, their limited resources, and their "lot" in life. They have a new freedom and a new liberty. They can begin to dream and to think outside the box. They can investigate new possibilities and explore new horizons. Identifying your ever-changing call will require you to begin to do the same, to investigate, to explore, to think like a lottery winner.

Just like a lottery winner, begin to ask your self:

- What's my heart? What do I really want to do for God?
- What's my dream? What do I really want to do for God?
- What's my passion? What do I really want to do for God?
- What's my joy? What do I really want to do for God?

These answers may point you in the direction of your new *ever-changing call.*

↩

Begin thinking and acting like a lottery winner!

↩

Outside The Box

I realize you will always need money. Every thirty days or so, your creditors want to be paid. I know how you feel! But I want you to do something for me. I want you to begin to think outside the box. I want you to begin to think big, really big, for just a moment. Remember, you've just won the lottery!

Just imagine for a moment that you won ten million dollars. What would you do differently today? Specifically, what would you do differently for God today? Now remember, I'm asking you to think outside the box.

I want you to see what's inside you. I want you to recognize that the call of God is changing. You are changing from the inside out. Successfully adjusting to your *ever-changing call* requires you to think outside the box.

Money is simply a resource. It assists you in fulfilling your call. It is not the primary reason to pursue your call, and it certainly should never be the primary reason you give up on your call. I'm just asking you to dream.

Afraid to Dream?

I asked a number of ministry veterans, who had been faithfully fulfilling their call for years, the "money" question. They all answered the "money" question alike. I asked them what they would do differently (for God) if money were not an issue. I was given some very startling responses.

> I want you to see what's inside you. I want you to recognize that the call of God is changing. You are changing from the inside out.

Without exception, everyone I interviewed told me they would change direction. With tears in their eyes, they told me they would change almost everything they were currently committed to in ministry.

It was the money that held them captive. It was their salary that they had to justify. They admitted they were afraid to think outside the box. They admitted they were terrified to dream.

Now in their defense, not a single one said he would run off to some dessert island and spend the rest of his days in relaxation and leisure. Not one of them wanted out! But they were definitely trapped in a religious system they had created. Each had failed at changing with their ever-changing call.

It was the money that held them captive.

Fill In The Blanks

Paul wrote, "Woe is me if I do not preach the gospel." Paul didn't play games when it came to his calling. He took it very seriously, and so should you. In essence, Paul was saying, "Woe is me if I do not fulfill my call, and if I fail to change with the ever-changing call upon my life."

You need to take this very critical test. Fill in the blanks of the following sentence.

Woe is me _____
                    (fill in your name)

if I do not_____
            (Now fill in what God is telling you to do, then do it!)

Remember, money is not a factor here. What you write in the blank may be the direction of your *ever-changing call of God.*

Again, what would you do for God right now if money were never again an issue in your life? Removing the money factor (at least theoretically) will allow you to dream. In the kingdom of God dreams still come true. But first, you must dream them!

"Regarding the ever-changing call
of God — demand often dictates
direction."

— *Dennis Cramer*

Question 4

As a Christian, what do people ask of you the most?
What is it they demand?

I n other words:

- What spiritual **demand** is most often placed upon you by others?
- What do others most often **see** as your spiritual abilities?
- What spiritual **activity** are you most often involved with — usually at the request of others?
- What spiritual **responsibility** do others most often want you to take the leadership of — sometimes to your own surprise?
- Where do you seem to be the most **needed** in terms of kingdom work — where do others feel you are the most effective?
- Where are your **gifts and talents** most required on a consistent basis? Where do others feel you do your best work?
- Where do you experience the greatest "**draw**" on your spiritual abilities?

A Perceived And Unique Grace

Paul the apostle said, ".... James, Cephas, and John all perceived [saw] the *grace* that had been given to me...." (Gal. 2:9).

These three men saw something "on" Paul. They became aware through exposure to Paul's combined spiritual gifts that he possessed a powerful apostolic calling. It was plain, clear, and obvious to them.

Your call will eventually be just like Paul's: It will first be plain, clear, and obvious to those around you. Then, eventually, it will be the same to you: Wonderfully plain, clear, and obvious!

This same grace of God, which is the unique call of God upon your life, can and often times will be more accurately perceived by others rather than by yourself — at least at first. This "perceived grace" is not a physical, natural thing. It is not a collection of natural abilities or skills. Neither is it a mere extension of one's personality. Not at all!

They Want What You've Got!

The call of God on you consists of the spiritual gifts and spiritual talents supernaturally deposited in you by the Holy Spirit. Then, this same Holy Spirit allows others to be attracted to this inner deposit, to these same gifts and talents. This is why they ask you to do what you do. They are somehow drawn to this call within you. The Holy Spirit in them reveals your necessary role in the kingdom of God. Simply stated, they want what you've got!

You're In The Army Now

In an army of actual, physical, professional soldiers, each man or woman wears a dog tag around his neck. It contains all the vital military information needed to identify that particular person.

The kingdom of God is similar in that each of its warriors also has a spiritual identification or dog tag. We call this "dog tag" the call of God. This "kingdom" dog tag marks the person as a unique, authoritative soldier in the army of God. Just like a real dog tag worn by a soldier, your spiritual dog tag identifies you, your rank in the kingdom, any special training or spiritual skills, and any talents or abilities you may possess.

James, Cephas, and John recognized Paul's calling, his spiritual dog tag. They perceived his current grace, they read his dog tag. The same will happen to you. Other people can and will see, perceive, or discern the gifts and callings of God that are on you. This dog tag, this collection of unique supernatural abilities that make you different from anyone else in the body of Christ, will in turn, make you very valuable in the army of God.

This is the fundamental reason why people ask you to perform certain ministry functions. They perceive the grace of God on you, they see your value. They frequently perceive (consciously or unconsciously) a particular gift or grace on you. Sometimes they even perceive it more than you do at first. All they are doing is reading your dog tag, they are perceiving your grace, they are recognizing your call.

So be smart. Begin to analyze exactly what other believers or fellow soldiers ask of you the most. It may be an indication of a new direction for your life and a whole new call upon your life. Don't miss it!

—

Often, others will "perceive" your
ever-changing call before you do.

—

What Others Do Not Ask

We have already established that you need to respond right now to the *ever-changing call of God* upon your life. You need to begin right now to carefully analyze exactly what it is that other believers tend to ask you to do.

You, however, also need to analyze carefully what other believers do *not* ask you to do as well. Both questions will help you to understand and respond to the *ever-changing call of God* upon your life

For example, from the beginning days of my ministry no one ever asked me to come to their church and teach a series on a particular Bible subject or hold evangelistic meetings, or conduct a worship seminar. Why? It wasn't my ministry, my gifting. It wasn't a grace that others perceived I had, and they were right! I am not a teacher, evangelist, or worship leader. These are not my calling.

What others "saw" on me was a strong prophetic gifting, grace, or talent. Churches asked me to come and prophesy over them. Why? It was my calling and they knew it. In fact, in the beginning they knew it better than I did! They "saw" the grace before I did.

Under The Radar

Many times your personal gifting, your "perceived grace" or calling will slip under your personal radar. You may be very gifted at identifying others' gifts, but you may have a blind spot regarding your own call. This is a common occurrence and one reason I am writing this book for you.

I recall the very first time a pastor asked me to come to his church and prophesy. He did not ask me to come and preach or teach. He specifically asked me to come and prophesy. He was very emphatic!

It all started when my home church had just finished hosting a weekend of wonderful meetings. Several other pastors, some from out of the area, had attended along with some of their own members. A pastor from North Carolina was accompanied by a younger man who was in his early to mid-twenties.

After the weekend of meetings, everyone was saying their good-byes in the host pastor's living room. All together there was five or six of us. The pastor from North Carolina was about to leave when he asked if it would be all right to have a word of prayer. Of course we all agreed. After a brief time of prayer, this same pastor spoke up.

"I would like all of you to pray for this young man with me."

So with that request the young man stepped into the center of this small prayer circle we had formed. We all laid our hands on him to pray. So, one by one each of us offered our individual prayer.

Then it was my turn to pray for him. Yet, I couldn't say that I felt to actually pray for him. No, something different was happening in me. I had this familiar "urge" to prophesy. I had never met this man before, and I knew virtually nothing about him.

As I began to prophesy the young man just stood there at first. He showed no obvious outward emotion. No physical response to my prophecy was apparent. He just stood there, eyes closed, and mouth silent. Then, after just 30 seconds or so of me prophesying, he began to react. I mean really react!

Slowly he started to weep, and then he began to cry openly. He was visibly shaken (in a good way) by the personal prophetic word of the Lord. You must understand I wasn't trying to solicit any kind of response. I certainly wasn't expecting him to get so emotional over what I considered a rather general, generic little old prophecy.

As far as I was concerned, prophesying what God had given me was "old hat." It was something I had done before. I was just doing what God told me to do. I had absolutely no idea what this prophecy was doing to this young man. In fact, I wondered what the big deal was.

Like many of you, I did not perceive the grace of God that was upon my life. I did not see clearly the powerful gift I had been given. My own "radar" had not picked it up very well. Frankly, I did not understand the magnitude of the gift I possessed. Apparently, others did.

"I Want You To Come To My Church And Do That!"

I finished delivering my prophecy as best I could. I felt I had properly discharged it and blessed this man to the best of my limited prophetic skills. I stepped back, and the host pastor dismissed us.

Immediately, the pastor from North Carolina spoke up. With great excitement in his voice, he turned, looked right at me, and said, "I want you to come to my church and do that!" He pointed to the young man on the floor, still greatly overcome with emotion at the prophecy I had given to him.

The pastor repeated his plea. "I want you to come to my church and do that!"

I had no idea what he meant. Do what, I thought?

Puzzled at his insistence I said in response, "You want me to come to your church? But why?"

"Yes, he said insistently, I want you to come to my church and do that!"

"Do what?" I asked. I had absolutely no idea what he was talking about. I was completely in the dark. All I did was prophesy a little bit to the young man. That's all.

Again, the pastor said, "I want you to come to my church and do that. I want you to come to my church and prophesy just like that over my people." I was stunned.

Why would anyone want me, a young, inexperienced and not particularly gifted or spiritual guy? I had never done this outside of my home church before.

"Denny Cramer, speak at his church? There must be some kind of mistake." He had the wrong guy — or so I thought.

Why would anyone want me? A young, inexperienced and not particularly gifted or spiritual guy?

So I continued. "Let me get something straight pastor. What you're telling me is this: You want me, Denny Cramer, to come to your church in North Carolina for the expressed purpose of prophesying to your people. Is that what you want?"

"Yes!" He exclaimed. "That's exactly what I want," the pastor continued. "You have no idea what you have just spoken over this young man. Just look at what you did to him. You've just totally healed and delivered this young man. You have changed his life with one prophecy. I want you to come to my church and do that!"

He continued, "And, I will pay for your round-trip airfare."

"What do you mean?" I asked?

"I mean I will pay for your airfare, and I will give you an honorarium for the week of meetings I want you to conduct."

I couldn't believe my ears! I was totally unprepared for this pastor's invitation. After all, this had never happened to me before. Why would he or anybody want me to come and prophesy to them? Anyone could do what I just did. It was no big deal, I thought. You see, I had not yet perceived this powerful prophetic grace on my life. The North Carolina pastor obviously did. He "saw" what I was unable to see.

Once your call is made sure, you'll have plenty of work!

Consequently, as a result of this brief prophetic encounter between this young man and myself, I accepted the very first invitation to travel for the sole purpose of prophesying to God's people. That was over twenty-six years ago. I have not stopped since. When God's people finally perceive the grace of God on you, you'll have plenty to do in the kingdom. Take my word for it!

"The purpose of your ever-changing call is to give you ongoing,
unprecedented access to the supernatural realm."
— *Dennis Cramer*

Question 5

As a Christian, what ministry activity connects you to the supernatural realm the most?

So what about you? Are you connected? Are you connected to the power of God through the call of God upon your life? Most Christians are not. They may love God with all their heart, but they are still not really connected. You see, there is connected, then there is really connected. Which are you? Are you plugged in to just 110 volts or are you one of the "big boys?" Here is what I mean.

110 Volts or One of the "Big Boys?" — You Choose

In one sense, all Christians are "connected" to the supernatural power of God because they are Christians. It is sort of an automatic thing. Since the kingdom of God is full of supernatural power, and you are in this kingdom as one of its royal subjects, you get power. It's that simple. Even nominal Christians, and even carnal Christians (1 Cor. 3:1–3), enjoy some level of God's power and gifting — not much, not the most, certainly not God's best, but some.

> *Even nominal Christians and carnal Christians enjoy some level of God's power and gifting — not much, not the most, and certainly not God's best, but some.*

Connected to the Supernatural

In one sense, each and every time any Christian reads his Bible, he is "connected" to the supernatural because the Bible is the supernatural Word of God. Anyone reading the Bible and accepting it as God's written Word, gets "connected" to God in a very intimate way. In one sense, each time any Christian prays (talks to God) he is certainly "connected" to the supernatural because He is talking to a supernatural God!

It is also necessary to attend church, pay your tithe, help the poor, and fast. All these activities will also connect any Christian to the supernatural realm to one degree or another. Why? Because all these activities cause any Christian to come into contact with a powerful and living God through obedience to His Word, the Bible.

Obedience serves as a conductor and a conduit that allows the supernatural power of God to best connect to or flow with our lives. Every time any Christian obeys any part of God's Word, a supernatural connection is made that results in accessibility to His promises, benefits, and blessings. So in one sense all Christians are 110 volt believers.

Obedience is the best "connector" to the supernatural realm.

Do You Need a Shocking Experience?

But I'm talking about a much higher and a much greater level of participation in the kingdom of God. I'm talking about more than just general obedience to God's written word. Studying the Bible produces general good results. Good results to be sure, but still just general results. I'm talking about going beyond His general promises, benefits, and blessings reserved for all His children.

Experiencing the full impact of the call of God upon your life is best understood through a clear understanding of simple electricity. The call of God "jumps" you from 110 volts (where most believers live and remain all of their lives) to a much more powerful, even electrifying level of supernatural experience! Experiencing the call of God upon your life is a wonderfully shocking experience that will spoil you for anything less supernatural ever again.

Are You a 110 Volt or a Heavy Duty Christian?

Most modern household appliances run on 110 volts of common electricity. Toasters, mixers, vacuum cleaners, and all other appliances use 110 volts of electricity to do their job. It's what you are accessing every time you plug in an electrical appliance in your home.

On the other hand, there is a whole other world of electrical devices that rely on a much greater power source than a mere 110 volts. These more powerful and serious types of appliances or tools require much stronger voltage to get the power they need. These are the big boys, the heavy-duty variety of electrical machines that outperform the 110 volts crowd. These are often the industrial machines.

While I was ministering in Canada, I drove through one the largest open pit coal mines I had ever seen. There, digging twenty-four hours a day and seven days a week, were massive, steel jawed front-loading shovels. Each was the size of a large house on tracts, and each stood as tall as an eight-story building! What a sight! You could drive four regular size pick-up trucks into each of their buckets alone. I mean we're talking big here!

Each of these giants were connected to several huge power cables, which ran from their own ultra-clean generating plant. These were electrical machines, not powered by standard gasoline or diesel engines. These massive electrical machines were driven by equally massive electrical motors. They worked quietly and without any on-board pollution to worry about. These were nearly perfect machines. Many thousands of volts of electricity were needed for these behemoths to tear and lift out the huge deposits of coal for which they were created.

It's the Same In the Church

You see, there are plenty of 110 volt average Christians around. The kingdom is full of them. There are far fewer Christians, however, who have the real supernatural power and stamina to get the job done. Why? They have not properly responded to the ever-changing call of God upon their lives. Consequently, they have become critically under powered.

A Christian who makes his election and calling sure on a regular and ongoing basis finds the true source of power for his life. He discovers a much higher level, a maximum level, a far greater release of this power. Like one of those electrically powered shovels in Canada, he is supernaturally empowered, envisioned, and enabled. He is more than sufficient for any task God may call him to carry out. He is indeed, one of the "Big Boys."

Which are you? Are you a spiritually wimpy little kitchen toaster, hand mixer or vacuum cleaner like most other Christians? Or do you want to be a highly efficient, enormously powerful, steel toothed, giant, coal-eating monster? Obedience to your ever-changing call is the best "connector" to the supernatural realm.

Do You Want To Be Really Connected?

There is another type or level of obedience, one that can take the average 110 volt Christian to this higher level, which is a greater realm of supernatural power. It is obedience to the specific, individual, unique call of God upon that person. This specific, individual, unique obedience to the call of God unleashes a higher level of God's power into a Christian's life. This release of special power enables the Christian to fulfill his call and to walk it out successfully.

Find your call, and you find God's unlimited power!

If you don't find and walk out your call, you will never experience this particular level of power. You'll go to heaven, but you'll experience little of heaven's power and authority while on earth. And isn't this what it's all about? Should not all Christians be living in the supernatural every day? The call of God upon every Christian provides access to this incredibly exciting realm — the realm of the truly supernatural — the kingdom of God!

Connected — Disconnected — Reconnected?

Every "called" Christian, (which includes you!), will experience a unique, personalized connection to the supernatural realm through his or her call. God's calling is always the connection, and your calling is always your connection.

Your personal calling is your personal connection.

What about you? Are you spiritually connected or disconnected? Do you recognize a deep spiritual need to be re-connected to the power of God?

Where are you right now? If you are disconnected, here is how you feel: You feel like you lack spiritual direction. You feel like you're traveling in circles spiritually and going nowhere. You are bored, and dissatisfied with your spiritual walk. Your attitude is: Been there, done that. You recognize something is missing, something is wrong.

You know how to read your Bible and pray. You faithfully pay your tithe every Sunday, and you love to worship God. But you feel lousy. You feel as if you just can't seem to "get off the ground" spiritually. You feel like you're in a plane, the engine is running smoothly, you've taxied out to the runway, but you simply can't get off the ground.

The problem is not the plane, the engine, or the runway. You are the problem! You just don't know what makes your plane fly. You don't know how to get it off the ground. You have not made your calling sure.

Ask yourself these questions:

- What makes me feel the most anointed — the most effective, the most spiritually connected in my life?
- What brings out my spiritual gifts the most? Where do I blossom spiritually in my life?
- What brings out my spiritual personality the most? What brings out the unique combination of spiritual characteristics in my life?
- Exactly where do I feel like my "plane gets off the runway and actually flies" — where do I feel I can really "soar" spiritually in my life?

Even The Sheep Know The Difference

Some years ago I was invited to speak in a church and decided to take a member of my home church with me for company. He had heard me preach and teach from the pulpit many times. However, he had only heard about my prophetic gift from others and was eager to see it for himself.

That night, I ministered prophetically to this church for about two hours. As usual, God met us in a prophetically powerful way. I spoke clearly and accurately to a significant number of God's people through the gift of prophecy, word of knowledge, word of wisdom, and discerning of spirits (1 Cor. 12). It was wonderful! God was so very good to us!

As we were driving home from the meeting this man sat quietly for quite a long time. I thought he had been disappointed or possibly offended at something he had witnessed. Actually, the opposite was the case.

He eventually turned to me in the front seat of the car. He had a funny look in his eye — a combination of shock and delight. I could tell he didn't quite know what to say. So he just blurted it out. "Man, Pastor Denny, when you get away from the home church, you really get anointed!"

He could barely contain himself. He was so impressed with the anointing God had placed upon me. He had just witnessed my connection with the supernatural — the connection that comes with every true call of God.

When you get connected, you too, will really get anointed!

What Was He Really Saying?

There are two ways to look at his innocent and enthusiastic comment. Either he was emphasizing how anointed I was as a prophetic minister, or, he was emphasizing how un-anointed I was as a pastor. Take your pick!

Truthfully, I think he was saying a little bit of both. He had seen the very real connection I had to the supernatural realm as a result of the prophetic call upon my life. Before, he had seen me struggle with a minimal anointing as a pastor — a poor connection. Or perhaps at times he had witnessed even a disconnection since I was so poor at it. Now, he saw a much stronger, a much more mature, seasoned, proven anointing on me as a prophet. He had witnessed a much better connection. The contrast between the two connections had shocked him.

The Same Will Happen To You!

When you finally make your *ever-changing call* sure, you too will really get anointed — you too will discover who you really are in Christ. You too will become connected — really connected. You too will see the spiritual contrast in your own life, the significant spiritual contrast between being minimally connected (functioning outside your calling) and really connected (functioning within your calling).

Your Spiritual DNA

Your call is what you were spiritually built for, what you were born again for, and what you were filled with the Holy Spirit for. It's your spiritual DNA, your spiritual make up, character, and nature.

Your calling will greatly effect your ultimate destiny as a child of God. In fact, your calling is your destiny as a child of God. It is where you will feel the most anointed. It is where you will feel the most connected to the supernatural realm. You'll always be truly connected where you're truly called. And, God's people, His sheep, will always know the difference between who is connected, and who is not.

"The ever-changing call of God on your life is all about taking big spiritual risks, and getting lots and lots of divine help."

— *Dennis Cramer*

Question 6

Part I: Where do you personally take your biggest spiritual risks?
Part II: Where do you personally experience the most divine help in your life?

L et us establish exactly what faith and grace mean in relationship to your *ever-changing call.*

First, It's All About Faith

Where are you the most spiritually *dependent?* Where do you feel the most spiritually *desperate? You've probably just found the area of your greatest faith!*

■ **Faith** is where you take the biggest spiritual risks in your life, especially within your calling.

Every call of God has a faith factor and an equivalent grace factor. Let's first talk about faith. Exercising faith is fundamentally a risk. Each and every time you "step out" within your call to obey God you take a risk. So in one sense operating in your call is a gamble: Something can be won and something can possibly be lost.

↩

Your ever-changing call is full of risks!

↩

This so-called faith factor is perhaps the greatest hindrance to you experiencing God's true call on your life. You may not be a very good risk taker. Probably half the Church is not. Still, it takes incredible faith to properly function in your call which means you're going to have to take some risks.

For example, as you respond by faith to your calling, initially you might feel:

- Insecure — uncertain and unsafe about your calling.
- Vulnerable — susceptible to inexperience and ignorance about your calling
- Fearful — the fear of failing at your calling.
- Weak — unstable and vacillating at fulfilling your calling.

However, you are not alone! In fact, you are in some very good company. Most men and woman of God in the Bible who responded to their respective calls felt exactly the same way you may feel — at least initially.

They too had to overcome their feelings brought on by:

- An awareness of deep personal inadequacies....
- The very real possibility of ministry failures....
- The constant risk of public embarrassment....
- The pressure of open ridicule and rejection by friends and family....
- The paralysis of loneliness, isolation, lack and despair....
- A life of misunderstanding and persecution by their piers....

These men and woman of God were kept dependent, even desperate for God. This is exactly what will happen to you as well. Your humanity and circumstances of life will force you to approach your calling by faith.

Your calling will always be entered into by faith, always maintained by faith, and always completed or perfected by faith. Your calling is all about faith!

But here's the best news of all. Faith does work. In fact, it works very well. Faith is real. You can be completely confident in this one truth: faith is the very real substance of the things you hope for and faith is the very real evidence of things you may not be able to see or feel with your human reasoning or five natural senses. But faith works. It's what activates your calling. It's how you fulfill your calling. You do it by faith!

Through faith alone:

- Kingdoms are subdued
- Righteousness is worked
- Promises are obtained
- Enemies are defeated
- Circumstances are reversed
- Weak people are made strong
- Cowards become valiant in battle
- Death is turned into life
  — Heb. 11:33–35

Faith is God's foolproof method for you to function successfully in your ever-changing call. Yes, it's a bit of a risk, but, yes, it really works. It works every time!

God, Himself, has given you a generous measure of faith. He has deposited within you the precious amount, degree, size, and portion necessary to fulfill your call with great success.

"God has given to each man a liberal measure of faith" (Rom. 12:3)

Faith will always over-compensate for your personal fears and frustrations — your personal limitations and liabilities. Faith will assist you to move ahead in God's call on your life.

Exercising faith to fulfill your call will always result in:

- Increasing Spiritual Boldness!
- Soaring Spiritual Confidence!
- Spiritual Perseverance!
- True Lasting Spiritual Effectiveness!
- Ministry or Calling Spiritual Authority!

- Permanent Spiritual Results — "fruit which remains" measured by the lives you have dramatically changed (John 15:16).
- Success, success, success!

God never calls a single individual to any task without first supplying them with enough faith. The bigger the risk God asks you to take, the bigger the measure of faith He supplies you with. Technically, you cannot lose!

You need to get excited! Faith is supplied with your calling!

Second, It's All About Your Unique Grace

- **Grace** is where you get the most divine help for your life, especially within your calling.

Notice what Paul wrote to Timothy regarding the relationship between Timothy's call and grace. Here we see that grace accompanies the call. *The call of God is all about the grace of God.*

" God ... saved us and called us with a holy calling, not according to our works, but according to His own purpose *and grace* which was given to us in Christ Jesus before time began...." 2 Tim. 1:9

Your ever-changing call is also full of a powerful and unique grace!

Be Alert! Your Unique Grace is Changing!

- You are going from faith to faith....
- You are going from glory to glory....
- You are also going from grace to grace....

The early disciples experienced "great grace" (Acts 4:43)! I believe the church is about to experience the same thing again very soon. And this includes you!

The grace of God on your life is changing. An extreme exchange is taking place. The old grace is being dramatically lifted. A new and more powerful unique grace is descending on you. A much, much greater grace! You are being altered, modified, turned around and turned upside down with a new grace from God. It is bigger and better than the old grace. You are being transformed, and you are evolving spiritually. Get ready!

—

You are being altered, modified, turned around and turned upside down with a new grace from God.

—

By Definition: What Is Grace?

Exactly what is meant by the term grace, specifically, the grace of God within one's calling?

- It is God's undeserved divine favor on your life.
- It is a unique supernatural empowerment based on joy: The Bible states, "the joy of the Lord is your strength." Each calling has a unique grace based on a unique joy.
- It is His divine influence on you, the medium through which God makes you a kingdom success.
- It is His goodness, loving-kindness, and mercy all in one.
- It is a dynamic, a working force, of the kingdom just as real as faith.
- It is the basis for all supernatural perseverance. It is the staying power of your calling.
- It is what enables and empowers you to be whatever God wants you to do and be.
- It is what causes you to be able to do the impossible.

Your calling is initiated through grace, maintained through grace, and advances through grace. Your ever-changing call is about ever-changing grace. It is the supernatural capacity to receive all of God's gifts, talents, abilities, unctions, anointings, and calls. Grace is what makes everything in your calling come together. No one will have the exact same grace as you. Again, it is unique to you. It is custom-fitted for each and every believer. How exciting!

━

I love grace. It makes my calling work!
It will do the same for you!

━

All Sufficient Amazing Grace!

Here is something even more exciting! The apostle Paul said there exists something called "all sufficient grace." I believe it exists for all believers — you included. Not only is the grace of God on you unique to you, it is also "all sufficient" for you. Amazing isn't it?

Have you discovered that area of service to which God supplies you with your unique "all sufficient grace" yet? If you have found your ever-changing calling, this unique grace, this "all sufficient grace" comes with your calling.

━

Grace is like a tailor made suit or dress.

━

Exactly What Is My Unique Grace Like?

Let's look at two analogies to better understand what your unique grace is like, the unique grace which God supplies for the called.

First, it is like an outfit made just for you. No one else could or should try to wear it. Why not? Because it was made (by God) just for you.

No one could wear your grace as well as you. Grace consists of all the unique supernatural abilities custom made for your ever-changing call. When worn, this grace will enable and empower you — and only you — to achieve the maximum results within your ever-changing calling. When these clothes are taken off, you will be naked. Let me explain.

Years ago I was leading a Sunday morning service. I was worshipping the Lord when suddenly something (spiritual in nature) just lifted off of me. It came off of me so violently that it almost made a swooshing sound. As it lifted off of me, I felt naked, although I was fully clothed.

I immediately asked God, "What is going on?" I did not like the feeling at all. No one likes to feel naked in a public place, and I felt literally naked.

I said, "Lord, what in the world was that? What just happened?"

He answered calmly, "I've lifted my grace from you."

Shocked at this reply, I spoke from my heart, "Why would You do this to me? Did I do something wrong? This doesn't sound like good news Lord."

The Lord replied, "No, not at all. You've done nothing wrong and this is good news. I'm just getting ready to put a greater grace upon you, a much bigger and much better grace. You're about to be promoted."

That sounded real good to me.

I remained in that particular ministry responsibility for two more years, with a diminishing grace however, until the Lord moved me on. Then I began to operate in the new grace He had placed upon me. A much bigger and better grace. A "greater grace." The same is about to happen to you. You too are about to be promoted. Get ready. Here comes your greater grace too!

I hear the Lord saying, "Your grace is changing, your grace is changing, your grace is changing!"

A Word Of Advice

Once grace is lifted, let it go. Another grace is being applied to your life. Embrace it with all that is within you! Without trying to sound flippant, graces come and graces go. The secret is to catch hold of any new

Once grace is lifted, let it go. Another grace is being applied to your life. Embrace it with all that is within you!

grace when it is being made available by God. This is a season when masses of believers need to "catch" the new grace being offered to them by God. It is also a season to let the old graces go.

WD-40?

Second, grace is also like WD-40. WD-40 is a popular industrial strength spray lubricant frequently sold in hardware and home improvement stores — far superior to any other kind of lubricant currently in the market. Men love WD-40. They use it to fix everything. I can make any repair known to man with a good roll of duct tape, and a giant size can of WD-40!

WD-40, as an effective spray lubricant, makes everything it touches work better, work more smoothly, work more efficiently, and even work quieter. It "fixes" everything it comes in contact with. It is nothing short of a miracle product. The more you spray the more it fixes things.

Most Christians know a lot about faith.
Far fewer know much about grace.

Spray Me, Jesus, Spray me!

I need you to get the comparison here: God wants to spray you. He wants to spray you with the WD-40 of the Kingdom of God. Grace is just like this. It will make everything you do for God go smoother, easier, and more efficiently. It "fixes" everything you do within your calling. It makes your calling work! It greases your ministry, it lubricates your activities, it oils your words, it just makes you do a much better job. Grace just makes everything work!

Find that area of your life where you take the greatest spiritual risks (faith), and where you find the most divine help (grace), and you have probably stumbled upon your ever-changing call.

I have been heavily sprayed with God's supernatural version of WD-40. It's called a prophetic grace. There exists on me a heavy layer, a thick layer, a very obvious layer of grace to prophesy. Why? This is my call.

*Your ever-changing call will supply
you with lots and lots of grace.*

So be willing, even eager, to take the necessary risks to fulfill your ever-changing call. This is called faith.

Then, learn to rely heavily on the all sufficient grace (the WD-40 of the Kingdom of God) which God generously supplies with your call. The greater the demand placed upon you by your call, the greater the grace placed upon you by God!

Success in the Kingdom of God is inevitable! Why? Your call is all about grace! Lots and lots of grace supplied by an incredibly generous, loving God who only has your success in mind!

Maybe your prayer should be, "Spray me Jesus, spray me! Give me all the grace You've got for me!"

"Every legitimate ever-changing call has a "price tag." What's yours, and are you willing to pay it?"
— *Dennis Cramer*

Question 7

As a Christian, what "costs" you the most?

You need to settle something right now. Your ever-changing call is going to cost you. It's going to cost a lot. In fact, if there seems to be no real cost to what you do for God, no personal sacrifice, no serious commitment required, it probably isn't what you're supposed to be doing for God. It's probably just so much religious activity — nothing more.

How can I say this with any measure of confidence without knowing anything about you? Simple. I know one thing about a true calling: All true ministry, all genuine service to God, all legitimate callings, cost. There is a price to be paid. A calling is never affordable. It is always expensive!

King David established this truth in 2 Sam. 24:18–24. David said, "I will not offer to God anything that does not personally *cost me something*." There it is in black and white: Your calling is going to cost you!

A truly called individual will always say,
"I will not offer to God anything that does not
personally cost me something."

From Personal Experience

Like you, I, too, have paid a high price for my ever-changing call. The price I have paid has been no less than the price you have or will pay. All believers pay for their calling with their lives. There exists no less of a legitimate payment that Almighty God will accept.

> **I have never met a truly called individual who was not willing, even anxious to pay the price for his calling.**

Here is a personal observation based on years in the ministry: I have never met a truly called individual who was not willing, even anxious to pay the price for their calling. It's as if God gives the called one a special grace to gladly accept the risk and to enthusiastically pay the price for his or her call.

The same will be or should be true of you. Your ever-changing call will be costly. We have already established this fact. But if it's a true call from God, you too, will be eager to pay the price.

In addition, your calling can also be:

■ Exhilaratingly inconvenient!
■ Spectacularly wearing!
■ Wonderfully disruptive!

For over twenty-six years, I have traveled extensively across the United States and to numerous foreign countries because of my call. Please understand that it has been my sincere honor and heartfelt privilege to do so. However, it hasn't always been fun and it has seldom been anything near easy. I have paid a very high price. So will you.

On rare occasion, as much as I truly love what I have been called to do, sometimes:

■ I have "lived out of a suitcase" which I did not like.
■ I have slept in beds I did not like.
■ I have stayed in places I did not like.
■ I have eaten meals I did not like.
■ I have been delayed in airports I did not like.

- I have ministered in churches I did not like.
- I have served pastors I did not like.
- I have been lonely for my wife and children.
- I have missed numerous family events, holidays, and just time at home, which I did not like.
- And, it was all worth it! Why? It's my calling! I was glad to pay the price. I was honored, even humbled that God would use me. Are you willing?

Do It With Joy

So far, God has yet to ask me how I personally feel about all this. He doesn't seem the least bit interested in my view of things. He has yet to ask me my personal opinion of His ever-changing call upon my life. He has never once let me complain. He has refused to allow me to feel sorry for myself. He has never even remotely sympathized with me. Why not? Because this is my calling. God knows it, and I know it. It is what I must do.

So why complain? It is His perfect will for my life. What more could I ask for, and what more could you ask for than for God's perfect will for your life? God's call on your life is his perfect will for your life, period!

Yes, there is a "cost-of-doing-business" with God — an ever changing cost of an ever-changing call. But it is my price to pay, and I do it with joy.

God's call on your life is His perfect will for your life. Why complain?

The Bible Says ... Or Else!

"Serve the Lord with *joy and gladness of heart for the abundance of all things.* If you will not serve me with joy, you will serve your enemies which the Lord will send against you, and you will find yourself in hunger, thirst, nakedness and in want of all things and He will put a yoke of iron upon your neck until you are destroyed" Deut. 28:47–48

Let me make one thing perfectly clear regarding the ever-changing call of God on my life. God didn't merely suggest I casually consider going into ministry. God didn't just hint I should enter the ministry. He didn't imply or merely insinuate ministry might be something I would find amusing. And it certainly isn't a mere hobby — something to do to pass the time! No, I wasn't looking to have fun, or begin a new hobby.

God didn't simply propose I serve Him. God didn't think it was just a good idea that I go into ministry. No, not at all!

He told, I mean, told me, to go into ministry — He commanded it. He spoke loud and clear to me on the inside — in my spirit. He sovereignly and supernaturally apprehended me for this one purpose. It was a divine summons with only one response accepted: Yes Lord! And I do it all with joy!

The ever-changing call of God in your life, although costly, is all about joy:

▮ A lifetime of commitment to Jesus = do it with joy!
▮ A lifetime of sacrifice for Jesus = do it with joy!
▮ A lifetime of suffering for Jesus = do it with joy!
▮ A lifetime of faithfulness to Jesus = do it with joy!
▮ A lifetime of obedience to Jesus = do it with joy!
▮ A lifetime of perseverance to Jesus = do it with joy!

Jesus fulfilled His calling with joy. So should you.

"Let us all look to Jesus ... who for the joy that was set before Him endured the cross...." (Heb. 12:2)

"Your ever-changing call will dictate your future more than you can possibly imagine. Why? Your future is not yours. It belongs solely to God."

— *Dennis Cramer*

Question 8

As a Christian, what influences your plans for your personal and ministry future the most?

Whether you realize it or not your *ever-changing call* has been influencing your decision-making process all along — especially for your future. Perhaps this has happened on a subconscious level at times. At other times it has been more obvious. Either way, the call of God upon you has been directing you more than you think. It is directing you to the degree that you even make plans for the future because of this call.

In one way, calls come in different sizes. So the greater the call, the greater its "size", the greater your future is influenced by it.

Do not make another future decision without
first consulting your ever-changing call!

Ask yourself: Why have I made the decisions I've made for my future? Why have I chosen a particular future path? Probably the ever-changing call of God has been a far greater influence on you (and your future) than you have ever imagined.

For example, my *ever-changing call* has influenced me, even dictated to me to make many specific decisions for my future. Sometimes,

> **Already your call has influenced your future. The greater the call, the greater its influence.**

these major decisions were relatively easy to make, and at other times they were very, very difficult. Yet all were affected by the ever-changing call of God.

Anticipate, Anticipate, Anticipate

Here are just a few decisions I made years ago for my future. These were all major decisions that I am currently living out. All these major life decisions were greatly influenced, if not dictated by God's call on my life.

These were not always fun and easy to make, as you will soon read. Still, I was obligated to make them to remain true to my call. In other words, my calling was the "constant" and my life was the "variable." God didn't conform my call to fit my life, He conformed my life to fit my call. The same will be true of your life. Are you prepared? Are you willing to conform?

God doesn't conform your call to fit your life,
He conforms your life to fit your call.

The *ever-changing call of God* on my life has required me to:

- **Live a totally debt free lifestyle.** I made this difficult but wise financial decision for my future some thirty years ago when my call was in its infancy. In fact, my entire financial philosophy has been determined based on the call of God on my life.
- **Invest tens of thousands of dollars writing and publishing books.** I made this critical "business" decision for my future before a single book was ever sold. This was a major step of faith for me. My call required me to write, so I did. This pure act of obedience was based solely on my call. I had no formal training to fall back on. God just told me to start writing because it was part of my calling. So I did.
- **Develop a comprehensive three level mobile school of prophecy.** I invested hundreds of hours developing a curriculum for

this school not knowing whether or not it would be successful. Why? It was part of my calling. My future success as an equipping prophet depended on it.

▌ Marry the wonderful, wonderful woman I've been with for over thirty years. God specifically told me this was the woman who would complete me and assist me in fulfilling my call. No other woman on earth could have ever supported me like she has. God knew! The call of God on my life even included a wife! Awesome!

▌ Leave two churches so my call could survive — two of the most painful, heart-wrenching experiences of my Christian life. Still, it had to be done. The call could not be compromised! I knew that a compromised call meant a forfeited crown.

Please don't make the mistake of compromising your call.
You could compromise your crown!

What about you? What life decisions, regarding your future, have been influenced today by the ever-changing call of God on your life? **Think about it.**

▌ Future money management decisions?
▌ Future education decisions?
▌ Future career decisions?
▌ Future ministry decisions?
▌ Future relationship decisions?
▌ Future church decisions?
▌ All other future life decisions?

All these, and more, can be greatly impacted by the call of God upon your life. Solomon wrote,

> "Trust in the Lord with all your heart [especially regarding your future] and do not lean to your own understanding. In all your ways [especially the future] acknowledge Him and He will direct your [future] paths." (Prov. 3:5–6).

Remember,

- Your thinking will be affected by your call.
- Your dreaming will be affected by your call.
- Your words will be affected by your call.
- Your actions will be affected by your call.
- Your life and the lives of those around you will all be wonderfully affected by the call of God upon your life.

"It's so incredibly easy to identify your ever-changing call. Find your gifts, and you find your call."

— *Dennis Cramer*

Question 9

As a Christian, what "gifts" stand out in your life the most?

Many times, it is a careful examination of your personal gift inventory (for example, the list of "gifts" in 1 Cor. 12, Rom. 12, even Eph. 4) that can help you to see what your greater calling is. In other words, within every calling from God there are many gifts from God. Gifts point toward calling. I want to say that again: Supernatural gifts point to your supernatural calling. Discover your current arsenal, your present inventory of spiritual gifts, and you will often discover your greater calling.

These gifts to which I am referring will be unique gifts — gifts that are "custom fit" just for you. How exciting! No two callings are identical because the gifts within your calling, although similar, are not identical. In other words, you are one of a kind. You are uniquely called and uniquely gifted to bring Jesus Christ the maximum glory!

It Started Slowly

Long, long before I even considered the existence of any real call on my life, a number of gifts began to slowly emerge as I prayed for people. Back then no one told me that gifts point to calling. I just assumed all Christians had these same gifts or at least had free access to these gifts.

I was a young and naïve believer that just believed all of God's word — a truly "childlike faith." So I went for it!

These supernatural abilities came so naturally to me, so second nature, so low keyed in their operation, that I did not fully comprehend their impact and power in peoples lives. In fact, I barely recognized them as spiritual abilities or gifts of the Holy Spirit at all.

Remember, this was all new to me. It was ground I had not covered before, and I had no one to guide me. There was no one to show me the way except Jesus. It was, and continues to be, a spiritual adventure, to be sure.

It had never occurred to me that the presence of these gifts may be an indication of something far more significant like a call of God on my life. I was just an ex-hippie saved by grace. I just loved Jesus and would do anything He wanted me to do. Well, apparently He wanted to "gift me" because He had called me. The same is true of you. You too are gifted, because you, too, are called.

No one ever told me gifts point ot calling. But I'm telling you now. Gifts point to calling!

Hey, I Do That Too!

I clearly remember the very first time I observed a real prophet minister. Prior to this I had never seen a prophet and didn't know what one looked like. I didn't know what one did — at least not exactly. I certainly would never have used that Bible term to describe myself. Not in a million years! This was far too intimidating a title for me. After all, I was just trying to be a good pastor and nothing more.

Remember, it was the very early 70's and every young man who got saved was trying to be a pastor. That's all I knew. That's all that was modeled for me. If you felt a call on your life for ministry you assumed it meant you were called to be a pastor.

After all, how did one try to be a prophet anyway? Certainly, I didn't know, and I didn't know anyone who did know. So in the absence of any real understanding of what a prophet was, I was just trying to be what I saw modeled in others, which was to be a shepherd of the sheep. However, God had other plans. He usually does.

100 Percent Accurate

The year was 1973. It was the very first prophetic meeting I had ever attended. I sat in total amazement as this man of God, a seasoned and proven prophetic vessel, moved through the crowd. Revelation after revelation came from his mouth. His impact was so obvious. Lives were being changed.

He stopped abruptly in front of a young girl and gave her a very accurate personal prophecy. I knew who she was, and the powerful personal prophecy for her was right on target. It was as if the prophet knew her personally, but he did not. He did this time and time again. He was 100 percent accurate.

I was immediately drawn to what I was observing. In fact, I loved it! But I was seeing something much more than just the accuracy of this New Testament prophet. I was noticing that he and I were alike — really alike. What he said to this young girl and prophesied to her was very similar to the kinds of "words" I had spoken over people when I had been praying for them. I had done what he was doing. But how could this be? He was a prophet, and I was a pastor. And I was a young and inexperienced one at that — a young convert just trying to help people.

Pastor or Prophet?

There could be no argument nor debate to what I was witnessing. He, the New Testament prophet, was ministering the same way I did. I was a plain, regular, run-of-the-mill-pastoral guy. He was a powerful and dynamic prophet. Still, I noticed our gifts of prophecy were very similar and almost identical. Both he and I spoke prophetic words containing revelation, direction, prediction, impartation, and loving correction when necessary. How could this be? He was a prophet and I was a pastor. I had a real theological conflict on my hands.

Somewhat startled, I said to myself, "Wait a minute, I do the same thing he just did! I do that too!"

Again, he began to move prophetically among the crowd. He called out another older man, again, someone I knew very well. This prophet then gave him a very clear word of knowledge. Again, what he spoke was so similar to the words of knowledge I had spoken over people many times.

I said to myself a second time, "This is unbelievable, I do the same thing he just did. I do that, too!"

He then gave words of wisdom, discerned spirits, and even operated occasionally in the gift of healing (see 1 Cor. 12). Each time a gift of the Holy Spirit manifested through this mature prophet, I recognized I had the same (general) gifts. His were far more mature and seasoned than mine were, but they were still very much alike.

Over and over again I said to myself, "I do the same thing he just did. I operate in the gift of prophecy, the word of knowledge, the word of wisdom, the discerning of spirits, and the gift of healing just like he did. "I do that, too! I do that too!"

The Holy Spirit was teaching me something very valuable, even life changing: Gifts point to calling. These dynamic gifts operating through this prophet all pointed to something greater. They indicated his much greater call. His gifts were a clear, unmistakable indication of who and what he was in God.

Allow me to be overly simplistic to make my point.

- If you have apostolic gifts, this may indicate the eventual call of an apostle.
- If you have prophetic gifts, this may indicate the eventual call of a prophet.
- If you have evangelistic gifts, this may indicate the eventual call of an evangelist.
- If you have pastoral gifts, this may indicate the eventual call of a pastor.
- If you have teaching gifts, this may indicate the eventual call of a teacher.
- see Eph. 4:11&12 for all of the above.

In addition, there is another list of spiritual gifts in Romans, chapter twelve, which, also may point to a particular calling on your life.

They are:

- Prophecy
- Practical Service
- Teaching
- Exhortation
- Charity
- Oversight
- Mercy

Plus there are the 1 Corinthians chapter twelve gifts or "manifestations."

- Word of Wisdom
- Word of Knowledge
- Gift of Faith
- Gifts of Healing
- Working of Miracles
- Prophecy
- Discerning of Spirits
- Diverse Tongues
- Interpretation of Tongues

Find your gifts and you find your calling!

So, as I analyzed all this, I said to myself, "Hey, wait a minute! If I do what he does, if I operate in very similar gifts as he does, if he is a real prophet, and we both do the same thing in terms of how we minister, then what does this say about me? Dare I compare the two of us? Are we really more alike in gifting and calling than I ever dared imagine? Just maybe, just maybe, I'm more like him than I ever thought. Just maybe I'm a prophet like he is. Is this even possible? His gifts pointed to his calling, could mine? Did mine?"

A Real Eye Opener!

This was a very daunting question for a young man to ask himself. Remember, I had never thought this way before because my experience and theology wouldn't allow it. This was all taking place over the space of about forty-five minutes. Truly, it was an eye opening experience — a major, major spiritual shift for me. This prophet's gifts pointed to his call, and this same prophet's gifts may be pointing to my call as well. My eyes were beginning to be opened.

Still, it was years later before the Lord publicly and officially used the term "prophet" to actually describe my ministry. Frankly, I was in no hurry to prematurely use a ministry title for which I was not spiritually prepared, and neither should you.

But when the time was right, the Lord began to speak to me through numerous public prophecies. I received these prophecies from many unsolicited and reliable sources, all confirming that I, too, was called to the ministry of a prophet. However, in my heart, I knew who I was years earlier because of the consistent demonstration of my spiritual gifts. Again, my gifts pointed to my ever-changing call.

The same will be, or already is, true of you. The discovery of your personal arsenal — your personal gift inventory — will indicate your greater calling, whatever it may be. Carefully explore, analyze, and take an inventory of what gifts God has given to you. This simple exercise will greatly improve your chances at accurately identifying your greater ever-changing calling.

Let me say it again: Gifts point to calling. They did for me, and they will for you.

- What spiritual gifts, graces, charisms, or talents manifest regularly in your life?
- What is your ongoing gift inventory: Your special spiritual abilities? Explore carefully Rom. 12., 1 Cor. 12, and Eph. 4
- What is in your current gift arsenal? What are your best weapons?

Please complete the following gift inventory. Fill in your current arsenal of gifts, talents, abilities, graces, and charisms. It is time to recognize and list what God has generously bestowed upon your life. It is time to acknowledge and respond to the precious gifts He has deposited in you for the purpose of blessing others. It is time to use it or lose it!

My Pledge

With all my heart, I _____ pledge, by faith, to release my gifts more fully for the purpose of meeting the needs of others. Therefore, I now list them in order to more accurately identify, define, and use them for the glory of my God! This is not an act of pride or presumption on my part. Not at all! It is simply an act of obedience. I do this by faith. I do this for my Jesus!

1._____

2._____

3._____

4._____

5._____

Through a humble and honest self-evaluation of your gifts, you too will discover your ever-changing call. I did. Remember, your gifts point to your calling.

Conclusion

Are You A Willing Servant?

Jesus was (and is) the greatest servant who ever lived. He said, "I came to serve, not to be served" (Matt. 20:28). In other words, this is what a calling does to you. It makes you a servant — an anointed slave. *Your greatest impact will always be in direct proportion to how willing you are to serve, to be a slave for Jesus.* In the kingdom of God it is not kings and queens who really rule. It is the servants of God — those truly called ones who want to be just like Jesus. They want to serve not be served. Are you like Jesus? Are you a true servant?

Jesus came to serve, not be served.
This is how He impacted lives.

Your Best Punch!

Paul served a multitude of churches over a vast geographical area. As a servant, Paul the apostle said to one particular church, "You are the proof or seal of my apostleship" (1 Cor. 9:2). What does this statement tell us? *It tells us a calling is measured in terms of lives served, specifically the transformed lives of both believers and even non-believers.* Your true calling lies where you transform lives the most, where you impart the most life, where you deliver the most truth, where you make people more Christ like, and where you land your best spiritual "punch."

What is your current punching power?

So ask yourself: Where do I land my best spiritual punch? Do I even have a spiritual punch? If not, then where can I get a spiritual punch? By making your "calling sure" you will discover your most powerful spiritual punch.

A calling is ultimately measured in terms of lives served, specifically the transformed lives of both believers and non-believers.

From Personal Experience

Regarding my gift of prophecy, people have commented....

■ "You have no idea what you just **prophesied** over my life. It was amazingly accurate!"
■ "You can't begin to know how your **prophecy** impacted me."
■ "I've never been the same since that **prophecy** you gave me."
■ "I've literally been transformed because of your **prophecy**."

Regarding my ability to teach others how to prophesy, people have commented....

■ "I received more in the three-day school of prophecy than in three years of Bible seminary."
■ "I am a school of theology graduate and have spent the last sixteen years as a pastor ... I have to admit I learned more in one weekend regarding prophecy than in three years at my former university."

- "I learned more about prophecy through this school in three short days than in twenty-six years as a member of my denomination."
- "Denny's school was truly inspirational, revelational, and transformational!"

Positive feedback is one sign of your true calling.

Apparently, I have a pretty good prophetic punch. Why? My calling is in the area of the prophetic — both demonstrating it and teaching it. This is where I do my best work for God. How do I know? How can I be so confident of this? I listen. I listen carefully to the people I serve — I listen to their sincere comments. Unsolicited personal testimonies like these, over the past thirty years, let me know where God is using me — and where He will receive the most glory.

The same is true of you. You will do your best work for God — you will be the most effective and the most deadly — where you have been called. You will succeed, you will be a spiritual success story, where you have been called. You will be rewarded by God, as you remain faithful to where you have been called. It's all about your call. Everything in your life revolves around it much more than you can currently imagine.

In fact, sometimes people will tell you where you are called when they're not even trying to tell you. Their unsolicited, unrehearsed comments about how you have effected them often speak volumes about your call. So learn to listen to those you serve. Those you have impacted might be telling you something very significant. They may be unconsciously conveying to you the very direction of your ever-changing call.

Timothy Was A Servant

Timothy was also a servant. Regarding his call and the responsibilities associated with faithfully fulfilling it, Paul wrote,

"I solemnly urge you before God and before Jesus Christ ... to preach the word of God at all times, whenever you get the chance, in

You will always impact lives the most where you have been called— where you serve the most.

season and out, correct, rebuke, feed them God's Word ... stand ready, don't be afraid of suffering. Bring others to Christ, *leave nothing undone that you ought to do.*"

In other words, fulfill your call, Timothy. As Timothy did just that, as he faithfully fulfilled his call as a true servant, he deeply and permanently impacted countless lives for Christ. As you serve others, so will you.

Paul's Was A Servant Too

Then Paul continued writing about his own call and the responsibilities it entailed. He wrote that he had "fought long and hard" within his call. He too deeply impacted countless lives for Christ through serving.

" I won't be around much longer, my time has almost run out ... *but I have fought long and hard for my Lord, and through it all I have kept true to Him.* A crown is waiting for me which the Lord, the Righteous Judge will give me on that great day of His return. And not just to me, but to all those eagerly looking forward to his coming back again."

Like Timothy and Paul, it's time for you to begin to transform lives again, impart life again, deliver truth again, make people more Christ like again, equip the saints again, and land your best spiritual punch again. It's time to get up and get going again!

Like Timothy and Paul, God wants you too " *to leave nothing undone you ought to do, and ... to fight long and hard, to keep true to your call.* He wants you to again impact lives, to again land your best spiritual punch. All this is accomplished through serving

So, Where Do You Serve The Best?

In review, begin now to ask yourself....

▪ Where do I permanently **transform the lives of people** the most?
▪ Where do I impart the most **life to them?**
▪ Where do I deliver the most **truth to them?**

- Where do I make people the most **Christ like in their character?**
- Where do I **"equip" or train** the saints the most?
- Where do I land my best spiritual **"punch?"**
- Where do I leave my richest spiritual **deposit?**
- Where do I produce the most **liberty and freedom?**
- Where do I operate in the most **joy?**
- Where do I produce the most **fruit — the best results?**
- Where do I decrease and **He increases the most?**
- Where do I help others to **find their gifts and callings?**
- Where do I make others **victorious and successful?**
- Where do I best **serve the Lord and serve others?**
- Where do I bring the maximum level of **healing** into peoples lives?
- Where do I instill the most **hope in God** to others?
- Where do I increase people's **faith in God, provoking them to make their calling sure?**
- Where do I do **my best work** for Jesus Christ?
- **What brings out the servant in me the most?**

Write It Down

This is the perfect time to make your election and ever-changing calling sure. It is the perfect time for you to gain the necessary clarity, definition, and understanding of exactly who you are in God today, and more importantly, who you are to become in God tomorrow. Your future, your destiny, your kingdom contribution, all depend upon you asking the right questions and receiving from God the right answers.

In "The Master's Call" I have provided for you the right questions. Now, go to God. Listen to God, and you will receive His right and perfect answers for your life.

So do it now! Write down your answers. Then be like Jesus, and be about only your "Father's business!" Amen!

Question One: As a Christian, what rewards me the most?

Answer:_____

Question Two: As a Christian, what depletes me the most?

Answer:_____

Question Three: As a Christian, what would I do differently for God if money were not an issue?

Answer:_____

Question Four: As a Christian, what do people ask of me the most?

Answer:_____

Question Five: As a Christian, what ministry activity connects me to the supernatural realm the most?

Answer:_____

Question Six: As a Christian, where do I rely on faith and grace the most?

Answer:_____

Question Seven: As a Christian, what costs me the most?

Answer:_____

Question Eight: As a Christian, what influences my future plans the most?

Answer:_____

Question Nine: As a Christian, what gifts stand out in my life the most?

Answer:_____

Have you been wondering what the next millennium holds for the world and your nation?

Are you worried that the Church's influence and impact on society will steadily decline? Put your fears aside! Dennis Cramer — in this prophetic pronouncement — makes it clear that the Church of Jesus Christ is about to enter her finest hour! What will be the impetus behind this great international move of God? His Holy Spirit-inspired prophets. Speaking and ministering with supernatural power, unusual authority, and perfect accuracy, these prophetic powerhouses will be God's humble instruments to bring healing, deliverance, and wisdom to the nations of the world.

The predictions for the nations allow you to:

- Look into the future of the Church and marvel at what God will do!

- Discover the actual locations of upcoming revivals by continent, region, nation, state and city!

- Gain important inside information about wars, economic conditions, miracles, weather patterns, population shifts, natural disasters, investments, governments, Israel, world religions — and more!

Is everything you do a struggle?
Does a dark cloud seem to hang over your life?

Are you trapped by feelings of abandonment and betrayal? Does severe hopelessness and chronic loneliness keep you paralyzed in debilitating despair? Are you immobilized by self-doubt and a persistent sense of overwhelming inferiority?

You may be cursed! And you are not alone.

In this startling exposé, Dennis Cramer details his 13-year battle with a "christian" curse and how God not only miraculously exposed the source of the curse, but dramatically delivered him from its devastating effects.

Could you be the victim of spiritual abuse? Could other Christians have pronounced failure and defeat over your life?

In order to bring to light this terrible darkness, Dennis takes you on a journey into the evil world of "christian" witchcraft, "christian" cannibalism, and "christian" curses—where you will not only be informed, but set free!

"When I read Breaking Christian Curses, my first thought was that every church should have this information."

from the foreword by Francis Frangipane,
author of *The Three Battlegrounds*.

It is an historical fact first century Christians openly
embraced and actively participated in the gift of prophecy.
They were a very active prophetic laity.

These were not just a few,
strange, unapproachable, mystical
"prophetic types" sitting on
mountaintops somewhere dressed
in camel's hair, eating locust
and honey, and hearing audible
voices. Rather, the entire church
body, every man and woman
who named the name of Christ
understood and experienced the
gift of prophecy. They were a prophetic people.

A similar prophetic movement among today's laity is precisely what
God is once again restoring to the Church. He is developing a practical
yet powerful Church in these last days — again, a prophetic people. He
is raising up a prophetic army, a prophetic nation to operate in powerful
prophetic giftings. The original prophetic purpose and plan of God for
the Body of Christ is coming to pass in our generation!

"Follow the way of love and eagerly desire spiritual gifts,
especially the gift of prophecy" (I Corinthians 14:1)

Dennis Cramer Ministries
School of Prophecy

Dennis Cramer Ministries presents a three-day mobile prophetic school — a new and exciting prophetic curriculum for the church of the 21st century. This dynamic hands-on prophetic workshop provides a solid, biblical foundation — a comprehensive program built within the infrastructure of your local church. This premiere training course is designed to release the gift of prophecy in the students' lives — to propel them to a higher level of prophetic proficiency. It is a "how-to" school which will forever change the prophetic dimension of your church.

You will learn:

- how to understand prophetic terminology
- how to interpret prophetic symbols
- how to discern time and timing
- how to "heal not hurt" with prophecy
- important biblical limitations and warnings

- how to "stir up" the gift of prophecy
- how to develop character and integrity
- how to practice proper prophetic protocol in the local church
- Plus ... a time of actual hands-on impartation followed by a series of prophetic exercises!

To find a school being held near you, or to host this exciting three-day course, contact Dennis Cramer Minstries at:

570.320.7757   denniscramer@suscom.net   www.denniscramer.net